HUSTLING

The blindingly real inside story of the netherworld of prostitution, the whole sordid subculture
of brutal pimps, Mafia businessmen, profit-mad
landlords, venal lawyers—and the women, from
ghettos and suburbs, who sell their bodies on the
street, at cheap hotels and expensive brothels, in
the tawdry whirl of the world's oldest profession.

"It took guts to write this book . . . there is a
street toughness to the writing that is gripping."
—*Newsday*

"A kind of Times Square peep show tour. . . ."
—*Washington Post*

"Realistic . . . brings the world of the prostitute
to life, real life."

—*Sacramento Bee*

Gail Sheehy

HUSTLING

Prostitution in Our Wide-Open Society

A DELL BOOK

**For women
with the courage to
believe in their own worth**

Published by
DELL PUBLISHING CO., INC.
1 Dag Hammarskjold Plaza
New York, New York 10017
Portions of this book were originally
published in *New York* magazine

ISBN: 0-440-13800-0

Reprinted by arrangement with
Delacorte Press, New York, New York
Printed in the United States of America
First Dell printing—July 1974
Second Dell printing—March 1975
Third Dell printing—August 1977

Acknowledgments

For their counsel and support during two years of exploration into the secretive world of prostitution, I am indebted to the staff of *New York* magazine— in particular to editors Jack Nessel, Byron Dobell, Sheldon Zalaznick and Deborah Harkins, who helped to shape various stories within, and to Clay Felker, whose uniqueness of mind sets the pace for us all. I am most grateful to Inspector Charles Peterson for months of free access to Midtown North precinct, in what came to be known as the *New York* magazine annex.

The special ear of Bernard Gresh, my research assistant, was a contribution equaled only by his courage in our street research. For introduction to sources within the *haute monde* of hustling, I want to thank Ted Buchwald. With the help of Paul Kelly's knowledge of organized crime as a former state investigator, the cooperation of Israel Rubin and Michael Klein in the Corporation Counsel's office and Douglas Hamilton's expertise in libel law, I was able to name the hidden exploiters of prostitution in New York. The immediate response from Mayor John Lindsay and Chief Corporation Counsel Norman Redlich were all that a journalist hopes for. They invited my cooperation in finding old laws and formulating new ones to inhibit criminal profitmakers at every level of prostitution; but more than that, they have stayed with the effort. At this writing New York City is actively beginning to clean itself up.

G.S.

Contents

Chapter One

Prologue ...

THE NEW BREED

A prostitution boom now—why? This is America the pleasure culture, isn't it? We're all grown up, sexually revolutionized and swinging to the point of exhaustion, aren't we?

Most people have this puzzled first reaction to the subject of prostitution. Considering all those singles bars and co-ed dorms and willing divorcees with water beds, one might be led to believe that prostitution is a dying art. But that would be to forget this is the land of social paradox. Prostitution is booming *because of* our so-called sexual liberation, because so many men have retreated from the free giveaway. Most of them don't know what to do with it.

Men over forty in particular seem to be suffering from a combination of symptoms brought on by the social upheavals of the Sixties: glandular inflammation and generational lag. The first has been provoked by a flood of pornography. The latter harks back to their boyhood training, a time not so long ago in America when men's sexual fantasies were commonly composed from nudie calendars in the gas station.

"You can't fantasize about your wife or girl friend," one ethnic-Italian TV executive explained. "The woman has to be an unknown." What he means is, women are either mothers or whores, which is the common state of unknowingness men have been in.

Until recently American men have had almost no source of information about sex. They graduated from being sons into being husbands into being fathers, never daring to ask the girls along the way specific questions for fear of admitting what they didn't know. The teachers were stag movies and cheap pornographic books. And then along came the soft porn magazine. Together with half the younger population of Harvard Square, many "mature" men learned the erotic gospel according to *Playboy*. To be good guilty fun the bedmate must be a plaything. A de-personalized no-no. All these young girls who say yes-yes on their own terms are, well, scary.

Today's liberated woman, forgetting that she is dealing with an ignorant, often initiates sex and expects her partner to perform. The man is no longer certain of being in control; he risks ridicule and humiliation. Beyond the physical demands, he must eventually deal with the sticky business of intimacy. The mature man already has a complicated life. Intimacy means more demands. There is also the need for anonymity, for satisfaction of transient desires. And finally, as more and more contemporary women require sex when and how *they* want it, they become

10

the very mothers of impotence.

A paid girl, on the other hand, relinquishes all rights to make emotional or sexual demands. She would never call his office the next morning and leave an embarrassing message. It is her stock in trade to *encourage* men's sexual fantasies, and exploit them. The man who is less than certain of his own "sensuousness" knows he will be safe in his old habits. It is the prostitute's job to re-create, if only for ten minutes, the ancient rite of dominance/submission that can induce sexual competency.

One of the strongest human instincts is resistance to change. A "John" is not some exotic social deviant. He is the politician whose ego is perpetually mauled by the public and needs discreet restoration, the corporation man who is never quite in full control of anything, the lonely conventioneer, the married man next door. All of them are given the same instructions by our society. To get approval, to get promotions, to get the woman, it is essential they "get it up." As our society grows more open, more urbanized and competitive, it is the rare man who has rest periods between demands that he perform as a peacock. A John is simply a man buying the nostalgic illusion that things are how they *were* when he was a boy. And so, as the supply of self-willed liberated women grows, it seems quite possible that the prostitution boom is only beginning.

Jack, shekels, mazuma, simoleons, Mr. Green, filthy lucre, even spondulicks—this is the other Why of prostitution. Profit. And profiteering is why this book is called *Hustling*. Surrounding the obvious streetwalker is an assorted multitude of major and minor hustlers, all of whom play their part and earn their pay directly or indirectly from prostitution. The cast extends from pimps, madams, Murphy men, knobbers, call girls, playgirls and courtesans to preying street hustlers and hotel operators, pornographers and prostitution lawyers, politicians, police "pussy posses" and prominent businessmen. And it includes, always offstage of course, the Mafia.

The stakes are high. Secrecy is stringent. Using the most current figures available, there are an estimated 200,000 to 250,000 prostitutes in the United States today. Taking the lower estimate, at only six contacts a day, and at the bottom price of $20 per "trick," the millions of clients of prostitution contribute to the support of the underworld the incredible sum of between seven and nine *billion* dollars annually. All of it untaxed.

The profit figure is ten times the entire annual budget of the U.S. Department of Justice. That fact alone would seem reason enough for tax-weary Americans to look more closely, rather than snicker, at prostitution.

The stories in this book follow the class ladder of the vocation. Beginning with the lowliest, jail-calloused street hooker, they end with the pseudo-aristocratic courtesan who plays in the big league for the highest stakes: wealth and social position. But before taking a walk up the class ladder, let's focus briefly on the second question Americans always ask of any booming business.

WHO PROFITS?

Prostitutes. It sounds unbelievably glamorous. Come to the big city and make a minimum of $200 a night doing what comes naturally. Work six nights a week while you're young and pretty. It's the fastest way to make money in the shortest time. How else can a girl earn $70,000 a year?

There are several critical facts the recruiter fails to mention. The average *net* income for a streetwalker is less than $100 a week. "To the pimp she's nothing but a piece of meat," says one police veteran of prostitution vans. And she ages very quickly. Prostitution is a physically punishing business. Right from the start a working girl begins to worry about her age. This is one profession in which seniority is not rewarded.

When massage parlors and peep shows broke out all over the playing field of midtown Manhattan, I began to see Puerto Rican faces for the first time. These were inexperienced girls of no more than twenty-one, sitting on the benches of sex parlors like scared second stringers waiting to be called into a rough game. I noticed they were all wearing baby-doll wigs and asked why. "The wig it gives me less age," said one wispy girl. She giggled guiltily when I asked how old she really was. "Twenty, but the men, they like eighteen."

The bottom line on the prostitute's profit sheet is this: the vast majority find themselves old at thirty, bitter and broke. In two thousand interviews conducted over ten years for their excellent book, *The Lively Commerce,* Charles Winick and Paul Kinsie found no more than one hundred older prostitutes who had any money left. Because prostitution is a criminal offense in many states, including New York, its practitioners are generally saddled with a police record as well, which demolishes their credit rating and further diminishes their chances of finding another job. They face the future locked into a day-to-day, cash-and-carry existence. Few of them can imagine where all the money went. The lion's share, of course, went to the next profiteer.

Pimps. "He doesn't do *nothing*. But the way he does nothing is *beautiful*." That description, coming from a starry-eyed beginner in the stable of a Times Square pimp, hits the nail on the head. She sees it as a source of pride. It is her earning power that allows her "sweet man" to drive around town in glorified idleness.

For this and a few meager services the street pimp demands his girls bring in from $200 to $250 a night. The girls rarely see more than five percent. Because of his neurotic need to prove total control, the pimp makes no allowances for a girl who can't meet her quota. One night in a driving rainstorm I accompanied a miserable streetwalker to a pay phone while she pleaded with her man: "I can't make but a bill [$100] tonight, the rain's sent everybody home." She got one word from the pimp: "Drown."

The prostitution boom began five years ago in New York when the state penal code was revised. Pimps across the nation tuned in as Governor Rockefeller appointed the Bartlett Commission to study "crimes without victims." Former Police Commissioner Howard Leary wanted to please his men, who were tired of acting both as arresting officers and prosecutors of the girls. In the fall of 1967 the maximum penalty for prostitution was reduced from one year in jail to fifteen days or a $50 fine. That was also the end of the Women's Court Clinic, where a doctor routinely checked arrested girls and gave prophylactic treatments of penicillin.

A hue and cry went up from midtown businessmen and the hotel lobby in anticipation of the new law. They warned, quite correctly, that New York was about to be saturated with prostitutes from other, stricter states. Mayor John V. Lindsay appointed his own Commission on Prostitution. It went to work on legislation to amend the penal code. And, as usual, this deeply complicated social problem became a superficial political football. John Marchi, the conservative state senator then gearing up for the 1969 mayoral race against Lindsay, took the stiffer bill drawn up by the mayor's own legislative office and ran with it. In the fall of 1969 "Marchi's bill" upped the maximum penalty to ninety-one days or $500 (still far short of the earlier one-year penalty). Prostitution was elevated from a violation to a misdemeanor, and for the first time in New York State it became a "crime."

Apart from burdening prostitutes with criminal records, the amended legislation was beside the point. Judges barely catch the names as several dozen street girls glide past the bench—"I'm a seamstress"—and taxi back to their territories to finish the night's work. Ninety percent of the loitering cases are dismissed. Only the arresting officers are held up in court, filling out reports.

Even girls who are found guilty on the more serious "pross collars," involving a specific proposal for a specific price made to a plainclothesman, are rarely jailed. Most judges let them go for a $25 to $50 fine— and a week to pay. Any girl can work that off in an hour or so. It amounts to a license.

Word of this leniency spread with great interest through the pimp grapevine around the country. New York was wide open. Midtown became the nation's largest outdoor flesh showroom.

Despite all subsequent "crackdowns," amateur pimps are still rolling into New York from Detroit, Chicago, even California. When local pimps have recruitment problems, they often cruise up to Montreal. A black pimp can always magnetize white *naïves* from Le Province by flashing his blister-top Cadillac.

Where does all his money go? Into "invisible investments": $15,000 custom-made cars which serve as floating country clubs (with false registration), a gypsy cab business, a home out of state, fenced clothes and jewelry, gambling at the race track, and to other phantom profiteers above him.

At the highest levels of pimping, very little cash changes hands. In the words of a white penthouse pimp, "You can buy anything with beautiful women."

Preying street hustlers. Prostitutes carry a lot of cash —temporarily. No one knows this better than addicts and muggers, desperate pimps and other competitive prostitutes. Murphy men make a game of selling dummy keys, for cash in advance, to customers dumb enough to believe a girl will be waiting for them in an empty apartment. Knobbers are men dressed as female hookers who have figured out their own ripoff on prostitution. They charge the same price but offer only stand-up service, pleading monthly indisposition.

"Prostitutes are pitiful creatures really," says a captain in New York's Public Morals Division. "The trouble is, they attract all the vermin—the muggers and robbers. If it weren't for the street girls, the crime rate would hardly exist."

Hotel operators. Fleabag prostitution hotels are run by a diehard little band of hirelings. They have no compunction about saying "I come with the building."

Pornographers. The link between pornography and the infiltration of a new area by prostitutes is firmly established. One promises, the other delivers.

In May of 1971, the Peep Show Man was up to his ankles in sawdust on Lexington Avenue, hammering in stalls that resembled make-do cattle pens. He looked like a hayseed Kentucky veterinarian. No one could have guessed he owned a string of twelve Times Square peep shows. But competition had saturated Times Square, he said, and so he followed his sixth sense to Manhattan's East Side.

"Only had three folks come by wantin' to know why I was puttin' such a thing in here," drawled the Peep Show Man that May. "Prob'ly be the first ones in to see it." And a week later there they were, one hip poking out of every stall, dropping quarters into the box to devour sexual images that have the approximate substance of shower-curtain decals.

Within a week prostitutes had followed. And what follows prostitutes is crime.

Prostitution and pornography lawyers. Lawyers who make their living by defending prostitutes form a small, closed, cynical fraternity. They charge what the traffic will bear. Theirs is a captive clientele. On the proceeds of prostitution they live very well, in the manner of legal pimps.

For all sorts of profiteers 1967 was the year of the double bonanza. While New York was relaxing its prostitution law, the Supreme Court handed down a series of decisions lowering the restrictions on obscenity. Within three months organized crime had entered the midtown pornography business. Right behind them appeared another middleman, an old breed of lawyer with a lucrative new specialty—obscenity law.

What these lawyers are really defending is not the public's right to experience imaginative forms of sexual expression, but the rights of property owners and mob-connected operators to extract maximum profits from the weaknesses of ordinary mortals. It is not uncommon for obscenity lawyers to have their own financial interests in the sex industry. Another habit they have is writing "public-spirited" letters to major newspapers upholding the virtues of civil libertarianism, letters as transparent as a call girl's negligee.

And so, while further Supreme Court clarification of obscenity laws is awaited, sharpie lawyers do daily battle in lower courts over the delicacy of police busts and the incoherent distinctions between hard- and soft-core pornography. In the jargon of the stock market, they are "going to the moon."

Politicians and pussy posses. For nearly a hundred years in New York prostitution has been used as the whipping girl for political challengers to flog political incumbents. At the turn of the century coalitions of anti-Tammany WASPs attacked the Democrats in power for their record in handling prostitution. Today Mayor Lindsay takes the same beating in reverse. Law-and-order Democrats use prostitution to attack a liberal WASP for permissiveness. One thing has remained constant: New York's courts levy punishment exclusively on the real victims—prostitutes—while politicians ignore the structure of commercialized vice which sustains them.

It is fashionable to blame the whole mess on the police. Politicians respond to the immediate public outcry. City Hall simply enlarges the expensive, demoralizing game of round robin played by cops and prostitutes. "Street sweeps" last only until the courts are choked with insubstantial cases and a louder cry comes back from the district attorney's office to the police commissioner's office: cut the arrests. Meanwhile, the girls evicted from one territory simply move to another, wait for calm, and return. And then the public cries "corruption" when the Knapp Commission reports that a few houses of call girls are sustained on payments to the police.

Why should a frustrated police force take the blame for a social problem the courts and the cream of city officialdom refuse to face squarely?

Prominent businessmen. Landlords are the one aspect of prostitution that has been almost totally ignored. It took me six months of research and roughly fifty pounds of documentation to put the names of landlords together with the properties in midtown Manhattan which housed prostitution hotels, peep shows, massage parlors, pornographic bookstores, and blue movies. And then I interviewed them.

The results, published in *New York* magazine as "The Landlords of Hell's Bedroom," were all very embarrassing. The names behind the booming sex industry belonged to a relative-by-marriage of President Richard M. Nixon, several of the largest tax-paying property owners in the City of New York, respectable East Side WASPs, members of the mayor's Times Square Development Council, Park Avenue banks . . . and at the outset of each interview, they had all lied.

Every city has these money-insulated real estate moguls. And every city to a greater or lesser degree guards them. It is hardly *comme il faut* for city officials to tattle on their peers, especially since they control much of the private capital and influence the political winds which keep a particular mayor afloat.

Mayor Lindsay, however, responded to the article by calling a meeting of his cleanup forces. As reported by press secretary Tom Morgan, "He told them to get off their tails and get to work." The mayor then graciously conveyed his appreciation and invited me to meet with his chief corporation counsel. In the first fifteen minutes of that meeting, the city's lawyers discovered powers they did not know existed. A law with plenty of muscle to make landlords responsible for their illegally used properties was right there in the statute book—Section 715 of the New York State Real Property Actions and Proceedings Law.

This law is only one of the existing statutes which can be used imaginatively. It raises hope for tenants and street associations in our criminally exploited cities. As they organize to battle the vested real estate interests, and their sheer numbers begin to register with politicians, the struggle may become less lopsided in favor of the moneyed few.

The Mafia. No comment on the profiteers of prostitution can overlook the shadowy but certain presence of organized crime. Who knows better the weaknesses of men and has had more experience in harnessing them?

Prostitution was selected as a profitable racket back in 1933, when the repeal of Prohibition forced Lucky Luciano to find new employments for the Mafia. The mob has had its ups and downs in the sex industry, but 1967 was a great year. Ever since the Supreme Court eased restrictions on sexual expression, organized criminal exploiters have been creating an almost insatiable demand for paid sex, both live and simulated. The demand still grows; it seems by now unfillable. Who are the mob's patrons? Everybody.

Prostitution, then, is many things to many people, from the street corner to the penthouse to the hidden realms of profit beyond. The one thing prostitution is *not* is a "victimless crime." It attracts a wide species of preying criminals and generates a long line of victims, beginning with the most obvious and least understood—the prostitute herself.

WHO ARE THESE GIRLS?

By ten at night they had the streets around the Waldorf ringed like an anklet of zircons. Horseface, Little Tiffany, Dutchman: the street names they assume are impersonal and sexually neutral, like their work. I first crossed their path early in 1971. New York was fairly drowning in prostitutes, and the excess had spilled over from Times Square to the East Side.

Money is power. Money hustled from the wealthy and respectable, for whom the hustler reserves the most contempt, is the most delicious power of all. And so the prettiest streetwalkers had migrated to the more prosperous side of town. Every weeknight thirty or forty girls at any one time would be strutting their competitive wonders up and down Lexington Avenue between 44th and 50th streets. The Waldorf Astoria Hotel was home plate.

They stood framed in the stone shallows of darkened office buildings like . . . cave art . . . fanning their quick, toxic eyes with double tiers of Black Spider lashes; teasing, taunting, flouting the public's most tender mores by turning men on. They traveled five miles a night on white gladiator boots with an apricot of flesh oozing through every peephole. Oh, mother! the frustration of those eviscerated salesmen in town for a convention who would dally with them in the shallows for one mad capricious moment before—before their pastry-laden wives would yank

21

them onward to drear little lovenests away from home. Today's street girls have no compunctions about approaching a couple. No time for social niceties.

Three girls would play decoy for the hotel's private guard while two slipped upstairs in the service elevator. They cruised the corridors of the Waldorf, knocking on random doors. *Hiya, sugar, want company? Don't say no or I might have to scream "rape."* The guest would panic, imagining his prominent name in the morning papers: PUBLISHER TANGLES WITH V-GIRLS. It was a $20 touch, work-free!

Zooming back down to the lobby, they would powder up in the mirror wall while keeping an eye on the ballroom elevators. *Okay, congressman, I'll be up after your banquet—just give me your room number.*

Minutes later they would be working in pairs to lure some simple Iowa Shriner up to a trick pad in the Belmont Plaza. *You take a shower first, sweetie, then we'll do you like you never been done before.* While he was panting his fantasies under the hot spigot, the pair would split. His clothes went down the air shaft and his wallet went with them because, as anyone knows, an Iowa Shriner is too moral a man to make a scene in the altogether. The wallet would be fat with cash and a wad of credit cards. What scores they could make!

For an average sting, a girl would have her John in and out of the Lindy Hotel in the time it takes to fry one side of a burger. A squad car would snake by. Gate time! And then the whole pack would be hoofing up Lexington and through the hotel lobbies and into the third furlong through the Waldorf garage to safety on Park Avenue, leaving the precinct boys in the dust again. Now smugly patting their wigs. Then waiting for someone to score a celebrity suite in the Waldorf

Towers. It was the wildest game in town.

What intrigued me was that these working girls belong to a violent new breed. They work on their backs as little as possible. More often they work in cars, with partners, and in hallways and in the open on sidewalks running through the theater district and surrounding the grand hotels. The bulk of their business is not the dispensation of pleasure. It is to swindle, mug, rob, knife and possibly even murder their patrons.

Petty crimes have always been associated with prostitution, but only in the past few years have New York's working girls made a habit of violence. Early in 1971 this new breed of hookers made headlines.

All within a month . . . a visiting Italian manufacturer was stabbed to death outside the Hilton Hotel. The beefy former defense minister of West Germany was mugged and robbed in a nasty scuffle with three prostitutes in a car outside the Plaza Hotel. Charles Addams, the cartoonist, was the victim of a particularly malicious act, also executed by a group of car-borne harlots. They stalked him past Bloomingdale's. He refused to turn around. Prostitutes, living in a permanent condition of humiliation, are hypersensitive to insult; the cruelest insult is to be ignored. And so when Charles Addams refused to turn around, the girls splashed burning acid on the back of his head.

Symbolic rape, it might be called. For in a crazy, incoherent form the message of women's liberation seemed to have seeped through to prostitutes. Why give one's body into the bargain when men go about crime much more directly? Why not attack the customer, take his money and be done with it?

I had become fascinated the year before by the sociology of deviance, particularly among women. At the time I was studying under Margaret Mead on fellowship at Columbia University. Dr. Mead warned that when women disengage completely from their traditional role, they can be more ruthless and savage than men. Men and male animals fight for many reasons. They fight as a game. They fight to show off and to test their prowess and to impress females. They have built-in rules which often inhibit final killing. Women and female animals, when they do fight, are fiercely defensive. There is no game about it. They kill for survival.

In 1970 the sudden violence of those women who were emphatically crossing the line from traditional behavior was not comfortable to admit. Dr. Mead's insight proved correct, but the statistics that backed it up were not released until the following year. We now know that women are becoming major criminals at a much faster rate than men.

Federal Bureau of Investigation records over the last decade show that female arrests for major crimes rose 156.2 percent. For men, the increase was 61.3 percent, less than half the figure for women. Further, the heaviest increases for women were in formerly "male" crimes: larceny, embezzlement, robbery and assault. The most shocking figure came out of the category of "girls under eighteen" (the age at which many prostitutes turn out). Their participation in "violent crimes"—murder, robbery, aggravated assault and forcible rape—was up 230 percent!

Traditionally, women have been associated with three types of crime: prostitution, abortion (when it was on the books as a crime), and shoplifting. The first two were self-induced abuse; the "crime" was committed against the criminal's own body, in the old masochistic tradition. But a girl qualified to be a house burglar, for example, found just as much discrimination in the criminal field as her counterpart who wanted to be a detective. No one would teach her how.

Toward the end of the explosive Sixties, men saw the advantage of working with women in revolutionary or criminal pairs: Weatherman-Weatherwoman, Panther Brother-Panther Sister, dope pusher and the addict-prostitute. Among the purely criminal pairs, a mutual drug addiction cemented many relationships.

Fierce women disturbed Good Housekeeping America in a special way. We watched while Bernadine Dohrn and Angela Davis, Linda Kasabian and her friends of the deadly Manson family, revolutionaries Kathy Boudin, Cathlyn Wilkerson and Jane Alpert, Panthers Ericka Huggins and Elaine Brown— all made a physical impact on their times. Yet most Americans persisted in denying that a woman could become an aggressor by *choice*.

The subculture of prostitution, I decided, was the place to pick up early warning signals of how women in "straight" society would begin to use their sex—and their specific sexual advantage—to push against our social boundaries.

Violent women are part of a much larger cultural shift. In contemporary America as it undergoes a slow earthquake of gender, we can see the awakening assertiveness of women most starkly at the farthest distance from the conventional center—in the netherworld.

THE HOOKER WITH A HEART OF GOLD?

That, I quickly discovered, is a male fallacy. Today's street prostitute can become as shallow, venal, and vicious as anyone drawn into the criminal world. She may develop a madness for money as intense as any corporation president's. Moreover, she can be *less emotional* than a man in conducting acts of personal violence.

All this opposes a persistent myth, the myth of redemption. For as long as one can remember, men writers have been romanticizing prostitution in wistful books about the warmhearted hooker they once knew, in films about the back-street girl who mothered them when their wives didn't understand, in plays about the chippie who fell in love with the nice GI and was saved. Perhaps these men were really writing about their own need to subdue women. For there is no more defiant denial of one man's ability to possess one woman exclusively than the prostitute who refuses to be redeemed. Most real prostitutes—contrary to the fondest fantasies of their fictional creators—do refuse.

They are also among the hardest people to get to know. To begin research on my story "Redpants and Sugarman," I went out to observe the game every night for weeks on Lexington Avenue during the streetwalkers' working hours: 6:00 P.M. to 4:00 A.M. I learned the rhythm and habits, the current places, faces and prices of the street. Later my brother-in-law alternated in the role of John or pimp. We compared notes with the actual prostitutes and their sweet men, followed Johns into the hotels and registered ourselves, ate badly, ran from pross vans, developed blisters, and soon felt as degraded and defensive as the hustlers I hoped to describe.

Saturation reporting, however, requires re-creating the characters' pasts: Where did they come from and why? How had the rhythm and habits of the street changed? What had happened to generate this new breed? I talked with all the obvious people, police commanders and assistant district attorneys, and followed the fraternity of prostitution lawyers from criminal court to their favorite hangouts; they were ten- and twenty-year veterans with an inexhaustible supply of hooker stories. But the best sources were the eyes on the street: all-night counter men, hotel staffers, newshawks. A stroke of luck was finding a retired detective who had put in five years watching the street from the same location—I spent weeks watching with "Bobby the Guard" on the Lexington Avenue door of the Waldorf and plumbing his memory.

"This is a rough street now," he told me. "Till last year it was a nice crowd, the girls. But these new girls coming from out of town are pulling knives and driving around in rented cars, busting heads. Say around four o'clock in the morning, if a guy comes up the street, five or six of them together will tear his clothes off and rob him blind." I watched it happen again and again.

Bobby the Guard introduced me to Dutchman, who held the self-proclaimed distinction of being the original Waldorf girl. She was on duty when the hotel opened in 1931 and claimed to have put two daughters through college on the proceeds. She knew everyone and was secure enough to talk about them. But every time a strange face slipped through the guard's door behind a male guest, Dutchman's antenna sizzled. "You're not going to let *her* in, are you?" the street mother would demand. *"She's one."* Dutchman said these new girls were giving the profession a bad name.

The real reason Bobby the Guard served as my best resource was because he cared. In particular, he cared about a beautiful black prostitute who went by the name of Redpants. I observed her for a long time and finally, through Bobby's efforts, she agreed to see me. The night before our appointment word passed like brushfire on the street: the other girls would cut her up if she talked.

In order to pull all my months of reporting into one unified story, I used the literary device of the "composite character." This enabled me to reconstruct the whole career of a prostitute from beginning to end. Every word of the article was true, based on police cases, interviews, personal observation and experiences, but the character of "Redpants" was a composite of several different girls at various stages of their involvement in "the life" of prostitution. An author's note to that effect was dropped during printing and the story appeared in *New York* magazine without explanation. Because of this oversight, the technique caused a journalistic controversy. The *Wall Street Journal* fired the first shot, followed by several *New Yorker* writers who lashed out at the "new journalism." It was funny in view of the real secret: the composite technique had been used and celebrated in the past by nonfiction writers for the *New Yorker,* one memorable example being "Mr. Flood," a composite character developed by Joe Mitchell to describe the daily life and operations of Fulton Fish Market.

The very reason that "Redpants" had to be written as it was provided another insight into prostitutes. They are threatened by all "straight" women, which in their definition includes all single and married females who don't charge. The superficial reason is competition. For every satisfied husband or lover the hooker has lost a trick. The more complicated reason lies in the prostitute's lack of self-respect, a lack so profound and pathetic as to make her fiercely protective of the little dignity she can command. Her weapon is to scare off other women by calling them hypocrites and meddlers, accusing them of jealousy and ignorance, embarrassing them with street language, and finally to defend herself by throwing her physical weight around.

These barriers made me all the more anxious to explore. According to Kai Erikson's theory of deviance, transactions between deviant persons (such as prostitutes) and agencies of social control (such as police and public officialdom) are boundary-maintaining mechanisms. Ordinarily, publicity about deviants provides our main source of information about where the "normative contours" of society begin and end.

But American women were pushing at the normative contours from both ends at once! The rise of feminism and the boom in prostitution coincided. As viewed from the center of our society, both groups of women are extremists. They stand in contradiction at opposite poles of behavior, with regard to men and their view of themselves as women, which pushed my interest a step further. I thought each might throw the other into clearer light.

PROSTITUTES AND FEMINISTS

The clash was bitter. When feminists tried to help, they talked in terms that had no relevance to the working lives or psychological defense systems of prostitutes. What they got in return were remarks such as these:

"They're trying to butt their asses into everything for publicity. It's hurting business!"

"They talk about prostitutes being degraded. These gals look and act like they've been recycled a thousand times. I'm supposed to call them my sisters?"

"What do these feminists have? Nothing but a lot of sex hangups and money hassles. Prostitutes are really the most liberated ladies. Isn't selling your body ultimately controlling it?"

Beneath the backlash was something quite different, I decided. Prostitutes are the masochistic core within all women carried to the burlesque. And they will do anything to suppress that painful truth about themselves.

As they lashed out at feminists, I began to see prostitutes as "masculinists." They are fighting to restore their earliest authority figures, men, as their natural superiors. This allows them to substitute for any authority within themselves—which they thoroughly distrust—the comforting fantasy that men are created stronger and smarter. And this makes it possible for prostitutes to shift all responsibility for their own lives, beyond day-to-day survival, to the strong father most of them missed and for whom they are still searching. By choosing the biggest, baddest, most brutish and dictatorial man they can find—the pimp—they are assured of remaining helpless little girls.

At this point in my thinking I flew to a great university to discuss prostitution with a feminist educator who had prepared a four-hundred-page thesis on the subject. She knew every legal fact—but she had never spoken to a prostitute. I hoped to exchange some of my information from the street. We never got that far. The educator began by explaining that she had approached the subject from a feminist and politically radical point of view. Her aim was to influence social policy by turning prostitutes into revolutionaries.

Prostitutes as revolutionaries! I couldn't believe it. The working girls I knew were driven by dreams of upward mobility that were as conventional as yesterday's American Pie.

I suppose that calls for a quick definition of myself, just so we have it on the line. I am neither a doctrinaire feminist nor a "new journalist," except insofar as I am inhabiting the second half of the same century and sharing the same concerns with those who are. I think of myself as a questioning feminist and an experimental writer. Anything can be changed by truth or inspiration.

Tom Wolfe, whose antic and singular brilliance I have long admired, wrote me a note after the publication of "Redpants and Sugarman." I quote from it only because it describes so well what experimental journalists are trying to do:

> It not only gives you a rich emotional experience, from inside the skull, as it were, but also more to think about than all the bales of prostitution stories in the past. Everytime I see one of those marvelous sets of wigs and boots now I say (most silently): "Hey! I know you!"

Form follows function. With "Redpants," hoping to convey as directly as possible the experience of being a prostitute, I went into research with the first-person form in mind. The function of "The Landlords of Hell's Bedroom" was to expose the hidden profiteers of prostitution, and so I turned to an old form of the old journalism: muckraking.

By the second summer I had gained a certain footing on the street, by virtue of having written about it.

Now the girls not only wanted to talk—it was a welcome switch for *them* to have a sympathetic listener —but they also were eager to teach me what I'd missed the first time around.

Out of respect for "Minnesota Marsha" and the average income she was sacrificing by talking to me, I paid her $50 an hour. She was a working girl. I was a working journalist. Time is money, simple as that. We understood each other.

Marsha repaid me with one of the most dynamic interviewing situations I have ever had. Once, at midnight in a restaurant concerned about its reputation, Marsha and I were asked to leave; the owner knew she was a prostitute. With us were Bernard Gresh, a research assistant and a teaching Christian Brother whose first date had been only three years before, and an Irish Catholic student from suburban Missouri who had already celebrated two "firsts" that day: he had seen Times Square and met a prostitute. He was about to celebrate yet another event—becoming eighteen. And just at that moment, we were evicted. The poignancy!

"I guess it's sort of fitting," Marsha said to the student as we poured a toast back at my apartment, "your meeting your first hooker on your eighteenth birthday."

He was enthralled. But Marsha was presenting herself in anything but a flattering light. She raised her glass to the two Catholic men: "Well, here's to the good" . . . then drank to herself . . . "and the bad."

Brother Bernie straightened her out on that one. He had already learned that prostitutes are as damaged and self-deprecating people as drug addicts.

By the end of the evening, the student was confiding: "I guess if you've never met one, you think of them as below human. She seems so nice. What surprised me was how she talked about having to be dedicated to your work, to make it to the top. But what happens when she gets older?" Marsha decided before the week was out to go home to Minneapolis to visit her baby and re-think her life. Brother Bernie announced a month later he was leaving the order to get married.

For one evening, that was a great deal of mind bending.

UP THE CASTE LADDER

Probably no vocation operates with such a fierce system of social distinctions as prostitution. The streetwalker has nothing but slurs for "those lazy flatbackers," meaning call girls. The call girl expresses contempt for the ignorant "street hooker." The madam wouldn't be caught dead with a "diseased" street girl. The independent call girl has washed her hands of the "bloodsucking" madam or pimp. And so on.

My research into the upper echelons of hustling began with an introduction to David the Pimp. A hairdresser friend, who had been raving for months about the exploits of this East Side Jewish hustler, phoned one snowy day with an urgent message: "He's in the shop." Packing the most inconspicuous notebook I could find, I bussed across town feverishly trying to invent an identity that wouldn't inhibit a pimp. I decided to do what I have always done before and since: tell the truth.

"A writer! Listen to me, sit down, you have the honor of interviewing the second greatest pimp in New York—" and David was off on a two-hour roller coaster of self-revelation which gave me an insight into pimps: ego generally gets the better side of caution.

I couldn't get David to *stop* talking for the next eight months.

My editor thought the story too undignified at first. One evening we were at one of those Park Avenue dinner parties where the conversation begins dropping off on the brandy tray like old bottle cork and by eleven the guests are backing toward the coat closet. The host asked what story I was working on. At the mention of polite prostitution, everyone woke up and exchanged vivid recollections of those bygone midnights that began with omelets at Polly Adler's place. "You must write about this pimp you know," they coaxed. That did it. The editor propelled me straight off to see David the Pimp.

We arrived at David's penthouse in full dress but without a scrap of paper or a pencil between us. Every fifteen minutes I had to excuse myself and dash for the bathroom to make notes with an eyebrow pencil on the back of a checkbook. (Without access to other people's bathrooms, writers would be nowhere.) To stay out of the reader's way, in the story I took the disguise of "the actress."

The most important thing to convey about David— the central fact of his life and the secret of his success —was momentum. He rarely slept and he never, never stopped hustling. Every twenty-four hours he repeated the same range of activities, though for reasons of safety and simple exhaustion, I never followed him for twenty-four consecutive hours. He kept me in constant touch through his three-line conference phone, over which I once heard David double-talk himself out of being killed.

The pimp's momentum held true during the period I was monitoring his activities, and immediately thereafter when he waved the story in front of Warren

Beatty and a half-dozen other dazzled movie producers as an affidavit of his fame, and then ran them all a merry chase. By the reports, it held true for the year he passed inventing caprices and peopling Beverly Hills parties for the deposed and perpetually bored king of mutual funds, Bernard Cornfeld, and through to his blithe escape from California in the face of a bench warrant for his arrest and $200,000 in jumped bail. David simply boarded a plane at the Los Angeles airport, popped out at JFK to shout good-bye from a public phone to his New York pals, and six hours later landed on his feet in Paris. His current girl friend (a staffer at a successful girlie magazine whose specialty was arranging for call girls to entertain advertisers) was already there waiting. They planned to be married. The only problem was David's two other wives. As the man said, he had never found time to get divorced.

And so when I wrote about David the Pimp, I tried to present him precisely as he saw himself: through a representative day and night in the life of a "twenty-four-hour worldbeater." The existence of a penthouse pimp *is* fantastic. People couldn't believe David was real, despite the fact that we ran three pictures of him.

My next year of exploration into the demimonde of hustling extended straight up the class ladder to the companions of rich and famous men. Let's stop right there and spread it out.

The street hooker is at the bottom of the blue-collar end of the ladder. She far outnumbers anyone in the business.

Separate and distinct is the whore-addict who turns to prostitution for support of her own or her boy friend's habit rather than as a vocation in itself. A persistent myth about prostitution is that most girls are addicts. This is not only untrue, it is impossible for a girl working at the competitive speed—running five miles a night, six nights a week, and turning six to twelve tricks daily *despite* rotations through jail cells and courts—to keep up the pace demanded by the pimp. If and when she begins to require enough drugs to interfere with her work, the pimp will lower her to bottom woman in the stable or drop her.

In New York, the quality and price of street girls diminishes as they move westward. On the more prosperous East Side, the merchandise is sharply divided into three subclasses. In class one are the daytimers who pull a steady bluechip business among Grand Central commuters, which accounts for their swelling ranks. They work the office buildings like a Schrafft's superhospitality wagon. Score the flustered account executive in the elevator, simple! Make a date for a "noonsie" in the office while the secretary is out to lunch. Discreet accommodations of all kinds are offered for the busy executive.

Daytimers can afford to be choosy. Haughty, white and businesslike, these ex-models and jobless actresses turn a trick for no less than $60. Their ranks also include bored suburban housewives who work primarily for kicks. With a few bills in the tote bag, they'll be home to slip the frozen scampi in the wall oven before husband plotzes off the 7:02. Enterprising!

Police estimate that ten percent of those prostitutes working the Times Square area on weekends are housewives from Long Island and New Jersey. Their husbands are mailmen or clerks on fixed salaries that don't pay the taxes on suburban homes. Since prostitutes are not fingerprinted, even with frequent arrests the married streetwalker can be home by ten with a foolproof alibi about her weekend activities.

"Got no pimps, these daytime dames," I heard a pimp complain. "They're no dope fiends out to support a habit. These girls make big money."

The early evening girls, class two among street hookers, scuffle in and out of the grand hotels until eleven and may go home with $300, even $400 on a good night. They are still new enough, plump-fleshed and pretty enough, to pass for wives on the arms of conventioneers. Many of them also manage to work independently. By ducking home early, they avoid the pimps and escape the midnight street sweeps by police.

After midnight the frenzy begins. The tough, the old and the desperate inhabit this third, aberrant class of street prostitutes. Pimps also send out their rambunctious new girls to prove themselves at this hour. Everyone has a gimmick. Or a habit. Or a car.

Next rung up on the prostitution ladder are rent whores, girls who turn a few tricks to buy clothes or pay the rent. They are independent but considered by their colleagues lazy and unprofessional.

Massage parlors, since their export from California to every major city, offer free-lance employment that appeals to a wide range of full or part-time prostitutes. Young, unskilled girls from Puerto Rico, Canada and the Caribbean are drawn in for lack of alternatives; groupies pick up money to finance their star-trailing trips; runaways and college girls are attracted to the tonier parlors operated by hippie capitalists. Massage parlors offer the advantages of an indoor job on a daily contract basis. Girls pay the manager to work and pocket what they can in tips.

The white-collar end of the prostitution business begins with call girls. Those managed by a madam or pimp may turn over as much as 70 percent of their income in exchange for Johns' names and an apartment in which to entertain them.

The independent call girl clears an average of $1,000 a week. She may have worked her way up, like "The Liberated Call Girl" of chapter eight, who is now happily writing her own book. But it is not uncommon today to find young call girls from wealthy families. Many seem to have substituted playing at being prostitutes for the old game-playing in drugs or revolutionary politics—a newer anti-apathy device. The element of risk is injected into a tediously comfortable existence. Topping off this level is the playgirl. She is a traveling parasite. Floating from country to country, executive junket to political convention, she relies on tips from the grapevine of jumbo-jet hustling.

Four common factors link most of the foregoing women. Absent or inoperative parents, an early and brutal sexual experience—often with a seductive father—an early pregnancy, and their resulting attitudes toward men: fear, dependence, rage. The rage of course must be repressed. To some degree it is sublimated in the process of exerting sexual power over men who must pay. Some rage leaks out, and it is this accumulated rage that is fueling the violent new breed.

A definition of prostitution that fits all of these women is given by Ned Polsky in *Hustlers, Beats and Others:* "Prostitution is the granting of nonmarital sex *as a vocation.*" But this excludes the woman who marries for money, as well as the calculated companion of gift-giving men who is, in Kinsey's words, "engaged in a more commercialized relationship than she would like to admit."

As Margaret Mead felt it important to point out, "Women are capable of prostitution in *any situation.*

They don't have to care in order to be sexually satisfying to a man, whereas a man can't pretend he is potent if he isn't."

HAUTE CLASSE HUSTLING

Under no circumstances . . . how gauche, such low-rent language . . . would one speak within elevated circles of a woman who marries, or who mistresses, one rich man after another as living by serial prostitution. Let us call her then by euphemisms.

Women who are in the *business* of marrying wealthy men qualify as cash-and-marry contractors. A woman who prefers to retain some freedom by moving as a mistress from man to man could be called an incorrigible courtesan. Although dictionary definitions of "courtesan" always include the blunt synonym "a prostitute" ("or paramour, esp. one associating with men of wealth"), at least the word has the elevation of a European history.

Certainly all marriage is not prostitution, and all live-in love affairs are not courtesanships. But most of us know women, and read about celebrities, belonging to that exotic breed who *plan* romance only with and for men of substance.

The distinctions between obvious prostitutes and the class of courtesans might be charted like this:

PROSTITUTE

Temporary encounters. She is selling her body minute by minute.

Noninvolvement of the John is required.

Demands on her are entirely *sexual*. Studies show the majority of Johns are "looking for something different."

Honest promiscuity. The first order of business is always to negotiate the price.

Erotic presentation on the woman's part is required to excite the John. Both are playing what Dr. Ray Birdwhistell calls "hyper-gender roles."

The male figure, in this case the pimp, *rewards quantity* of sexual contacts

COURTESAN

Permanent or serial relationships are the goal.

Commitment by the lover or husband is desired.

Demands are often primarily *social*. The rich man wants a good hostess, an intelligent companion, a flattering accessory. He may also want to be free of sexual obligations.

Façade of fidelity over serial promiscuity. The man cooperates; he does not want to know about her past.

Respectable presentation is essential to protect the man from ridicule. As Sheilah Graham points out, "The American women who pick off the best men are careful to maintain an impeccable reputation."

The male figure, the courtesan's "protector," *rewards exclusively* by

PROSTITUTE	COURTESAN
by promoting the woman to "wife" in his stable.	providing her with a place to live, gifts and security.
Irresponsibility. The prostitute holds herself accountable only for day-to-day survival; she leaves the planning and execution of her life goals to the pimp.	*Discipline.* The courtesan is capable of postponing gratification with an eye to achieving her own longer-term goals.

The thread of continuity connecting both kinds of behavior is that these women neither see themselves nor require that other people see them as people. They are willing commodities. They live their personal and professional lives by openly seeking or by cleverly insinuating themselves into a man's wallet. To the men in their lives both are possessions. The prostitute is a temporary purchase, to be enjoyed like a bottle of wine and thrown away. The courtesan is a possession to keep (at least until he becomes bored), a beautiful sculpture to admire behind closed doors or to display as a prestige item.

Sheilah Graham, who was F. Scott Fitzgerald's mistress, operated by her own admission an imperfect courtesan. Yet in her memoir, *A State of Heat,* she acknowledges the essential qualities shared by women who are successful in the business of marrying rich men. To be made of steel, she says, has stood Jacqueline Onassis in good stead. To be "a cool customer who, beneath her helpless, charming façade, pursues what she wants relentlessly," is how she describes the iron butterfly who acquired, after a series of generous lovers and two rich and famous husbands, one of the wealthiest widowers in America. But the most vital quality is the one courtesan Graham admits lacking: discipline. "My own chief problem has been that I am not disciplined enough to wait for what I want," she writes. "I want it *now*."

In her chronicle of dignified women who use sex to get what they want, Sheilah Graham admits to another flaw that is never to be found among the iron ladies of this circle. She prefers to spend her own money—even to work for it. When she had to ask her husband for taxi money, she yearned to be independent again. But to the women who descend on New York sniffing in dead earnest for old family fortunes, the hunt is all-consuming. A job would divert their energies. And more to the point, a courtesan is selling her *de*pendence. She communicates: "Protect me. I'm defenseless. I need you." To work is heresy!

It is not enough to be pretty, charming, graceful, impeccably dressed and talented in the arts of hostessing and listening, as are all the celebrated courtesans of our day. To collect millionaires and gather from them convertible assets, these women must also develop imaginative devices.

Pump-priming. A femme fatale well known to TV audiences often uses this technique the morning after she first allows a man to spend the night. She heads straight for Tiffany's to buy him a gold cigarette case. She has it inscribed with a sentiment both flattering and tastefully torrid, such as: "Thank you, darling, for one of the most memorable evenings of love in my life." The man receives this wildly expensive gift for doing nothing more than taking her to bed. If her pump-priming works, he responds with a $25,000 necklace from Harry Winston.

Party-prowling. Certain enterprising bachelors in New York—basically salesmen with big titles in luxury businesses such as jewelry—are counted on by tycoons to give parties for the purpose of introducing them to the beautiful new girls in town. The businesslike courtesan not only gets herself on the guest list, she asks the right questions of the right middleman. One evening at such a party, a ripening Roman beauty caught the ear of a well-connected public relations man. She explained that she and her prospect, a famous industrialist whose divorce was not incipient enough to suit her, had had a fight that day. "It's not going to work with him," she said flatly, and without skipping a sentimental beat, followed up with the simple question: "What other rich men do you know who I can marry?"

Jewelry-converting. An executive salesman for one of Fifth Avenue's most exclusive diamond emporiums always advised cash-and-marry contractors, "Get these men to give you jewelry. If you ever fall on hard times, we'll be glad to buy the pieces back." The biggest coup was carried off by the wife of a stock market swindler. She knew, a few days before the market did, that the bottom was about to fall out of her husband's company. While he was staging a last fight to save the stock, she bounced into the diamond store and charged a half million or so worth of jewels. Her husband did go broke and fled to Brazil. She sold the baubles back to the store. But this time the trick was too blatant. The executive salesman was caught, and with him the acquisitive wife, whose trouble was being in too much of a hurry.

Collecting tangibles. With an eye toward providing her own security in advancing age, the incorrigible courtesan taps her men for tangible, convertible gifts. Rented living quarters, no matter how sumptuous, are considered wholly undesirable. "They ask for a small pied-à-terre, and then shop for priceless antiques to fill it," says a Manhattan real estate agent accustomed to finding accommodations for the mistresses of her luxury clientele. "The antiques belong to them, they're salable!" Other convertible gifts are paintings, objets d'art, a co-op apartment, a piece of land, a country house.

In the process of collecting all these things on her breathtaking passage through the lives of affluent European lovers and American husbands, one envied courtesan became skilled at selling the right assets at the most propitious time. She had learned that with any less business acumen, the courtesan between lovers may find herself in a "sensitive cash-flow position." This is not only embarrassing, it's unattractive *and* suspicious. On reaching her mid-forties, she had consolidated all the gifts into her own estate—an exquisitely appointed home and many accumulated acres to go with it. When a supermillionaire suddenly became available, he saw her as a member of his own rarified circle. He offered a marriage contract settling on her a sum appropriate to her position—ten million dollars.

Inventing occasions. "What kind of party shall we have for my birthday?" Or, "Look at the calendar, darling, we'll be married a month on Saturday!" Or, "It's almost a year since our first evening together, and I'm so sentimental—how shall we celebrate?" After the marriage, a frequent visitor in the home of a former courtesan was baffled by hearing her constantly float such ideas in the presence of guests. Another wealthy woman explained. It's a way of inventing occasions for which her husband will feel obliged to buy her a present.

Name-saving. After the divorce, a lady who carried the name of an aristocratic American family, revered almost as royalty, never remarried. Bystanders were baffled. She took one famous lover in the domestic film industry and drove another lover to drink himself out of the British cabinet. But she would not marry. She was not about to erase the one asset on which she could always trade—her former husband's name.

The final story brings us full range from the streetwalker Redpants, who opens the book, to the zenith of polite hustling for "The Ultimate Trick." Only in these two stories are the main characters fictionalized. The widow in "The Ultimate Trick" is a composite of several women, and the quotes, anecdotes and supporting cast are assembled from several years of acquaintance with their lives. The form is literary. The function is to present the life style while protecting the privacy of perfectly decent people.

We Americans are famous for institutionalizing our social and moral hypocrisies: the polite unemployed, spongers on the rich, are called playboys; the culturebound poor, applying for public relief, are called welfare loafers. We often acknowledge such riddles in politics, law and ordinary business life. But we generally miss similar deceptions when they veil the activities of people in a less familiar world—the baffling, secretive, conniving netherworld.

My point is that when applied to the multibillion-dollar business of hustling, our great moral hypocrisies again break down according to class lines. Prostitutes are not laughable social deviants. They are women operating at every level of a consumer society who too often begin with a baby-sitting problem and end as throwaway human beings.

Excepting China, there is no civilized country in the world without prostitution. But only in America is the prostitute punished for prostitution per se—the barter of sex for money—and often she is punished by the same men who after hours seek her favors. Very little thought has been applied to tackling, or even taxing, the real profiteers. Even less thought has been given to creative experiments in rehabilitating the prostitute.

The deep social and criminal puzzles surrounding the prostitution boom are not a "New York problem," any more than this is a "New York book."

What we are seeing today in New York—as well as in San Francisco, New Orleans and all the other cities where mayors are screaming about the same cynical exploitation of our civil liberties—is the *criminalization* of prostitution and pornography. On the street both attract criminals, generate crimes with real victims, subvert honest policemen, demoralize legitimate businessmen and veil problems much more serious than most people seem willing to face. Like many others, I applauded those civil libertarians in the Sixties who defended our right to see *Oh! Calcutta!*, read Ralph Ginzburg's magazines and watch Lenny Bruce in a nightclub. I have no objection to people in the privacy of their homes watching a porno movie in the company of a naked puma. But things have changed.

For every latter-day belly dancer on Bourbon Street or street pross on Eighth Avenue, there follow probably three addicts, a dozen ripoff artists and marginal hustlers, a fleabag hotel or massage parlor operator, in some cases a Mafia protection man, and always a pimp. The struggle against big-city street prostitution and blatant pornography is not a bluenoser's battle against sexual liberation. It is a battle against crime of the rankest kind. If it is lost, then legitimate businesses, tourists, frightened residents and probably the last of the middle class will flee our urban centers. Tax bases will dry up and the luck of the cities will finally run out.

We have to make our own luck. To that end, I would suggest that the Constitution is not a suicide pact.

Chapter Two

It was a nonmarriage made in hell and
played out for money, in the summers
of 1970-1971, when prostitution found a
new street and violence followed . . .
He made her a Waldorf girl and she made
him $400 a night. Their stable was the
envy of Lexington Avenue until money
got the better of . . .

REDPANTS
AND SUGARMAN

Business is off tonight for the Waldorf girls. The long
holiday weekend dried up the street; weekends always
do on this side of town because the Waldorf girls work
the sort of trade who can afford to escape. It is Tues-
day now. Unseasonably cold. The girls are out seven
to a corner with some catching up to do. Their pimps
are itchy. Beneath the volatile skin of the street a new
savagery can be felt, like a contagion along the nerves.

The girl in red pants ducks into the Belmont Plaza
all-night drugstore.

"Got a hammer? My heel came off in a chase."

She is thin as a needle, tracked in the arms and
urgent around the eyes. The druggist produces a hammer. She lifts one long, exquisitely bolted leg in an
arabesque—every eye in the store bleeds because her

legs are still dazzling—and she says to the druggist, "Tap it on for me, will you, sugar?"

She is wearing Gucci shoes. Remnants of a near past when the girl they called Redpants lit up this street like fireworks.

"My old man was so nice to me the last four days," murmurs the pallid East Village runaway with her. She is sixteen and her face is blank as a cabbage. "No fights, nothing but loving because there was no work to be done." The runaway gathers an orange tabby cat in her arms up close to her Pucci nightie. "I didn't ever want to come back to work."

Redpants, who has taken it upon herself to break in this baby runaway, fixes her with the cold eye of experience. "Your old man won't be so nice when he picks you up at four. Unless you're ready with the only kind of loving the pimp knows."

"What's that?"

"Mr. Green."

Outside, the woman and her young companion quickly return to a tacky Chevrolet parked a few blocks down from the Waldorf, but they do not get in. They lean against it, bare-legged.

After midnight now: this is the hour one can feel the skin of the street break. Only the retreads and the riffraff and the hard-core dopies are out now. The Queen of the Pickpockets, a dried breadcrust of a woman, is in position on the steps of the Belmont Plaza waiting for a mark. Farther down the street, cruising, is the seventy-two-year-old Madam, another fixture. She is out with her single surviving protégé, who is forty, and who does the work after the indefatigable Madam does the talking. Yelps are beginning to echo from the side streets. The pimps have begun to discipline those deemed lazy by cuffing them around.

But what's on the street tonight, Daddy? Nothing but dipsy drunks, cheapskate metal men booked into the Waldorf with their wives, pathetic little studdies in from Brooklyn to show off their eye makeup . . . and cops.

Only the car girls are scoring. They play mean.

"Don't go out there now, friend," Bobby the Guard warns a Waldorf guest who has had too much to drink but not enough action. The Bull and Bear closes early these nights. Even in the ballroom the after-midnight sound is a hum of institutional vacuum cleaners. Recession is keeping most people away, and fear of crime in the streets. But not this live wire.

"I can take care of myself." He is a retired detective from Florida and as he points out: *they're only women.*

Bobby smiles. "When you get in one of those cars, mister, you goin' to have a busted head."

Ten minutes later the old Madam and a couple of traditional foot girls stop by Bobby the Guard's door to chat. A sound causes them to stiffen. A car horn smears its cry for help all over the territory.

"Uh-oh, they must of rolled the wrong John," the Madam says.

"I told him but they won't listen," Bobby says.

Of course it is the former Florida detective, pinned in a car between two prostitutes, one of whom is arousing him while the other is picking his pocket. The man, however, has discovered the game; he is leaning on the car horn for all he is worth.

"Here come the poh-leece." A sense signal passes from corner to corner. Well before an actual siren answers the car horn, the foot girls are sprinting for their hideaway in the Waldorf garage.

The tacky Chevrolet squeals into the same garage.

In a blur of speed a woman and her companion abandon the car, leaving its doors to hang dizzily open. A
few seconds behind, on foot, follows the former Florida detective. A slug of flesh is bitten out of his cheek.

One of the car girls darts through the back lobby of
her old stamping ground. Without missing a beat,
poised to whirl through the brass-trimmed door onto
Lexington, she kicks off the Gucci shoes at Bobby the
Guard's feet.

"Redpants, that you?" His voice leaps.

"Hold my shoes!"

No time for nostalgia. A younger girl flees past Bobby and drops something black. Traveler's checks. As
he bends to retrieve them, a man's arm sheathed in
chocolate net scoops under his nose and grabs the
checkbook. And then the pimp is gone too.

By now police are swarming through the garage.
They smoke out all the wrong girls, any girls, and pile
them into the squad car. Another squad car is filling
up on Lexington. One face turns and through the rear
window catches the guard's uncertain, hopeful eye.
Redpants blows a kiss.

Bobby the Guard stoops for the shoes she kicked
off. He runs a hand over the pitted soles. The relief
man, a new man, is waiting for him to go home.
Oblivious, Bobby stares past the brass-trimmed door
into the street which is now still. His cheeks are damp.

"She was the prettiest brown-skinned girl I ever
seen on the street."

The relief man is about to laugh but something in
Bobby's voice holds him back.

"When I came on here three years ago everybody
was talkin' about Redpants," Bobby says. "She was
tall as a tree and she had a shape and she was beautiful. Bought everybody presents too. I mean Redpants,

she was makin' so much money she didn't know what to do with it."

The relief man says she didn't look so good tonight.

"You wouldn't either!" Bobby snaps. "After two years on the street, runnin' from the cops, climbin' these stairs, livin' on hot dogs, they decline. They finish. Pimp took alla Redpants' money. Now she's thirty. She hasn't got no money, she hasn't got no looks, she hasn't got no shape, so she's just out there as a scavenger. She's done."

Bobby rolls up Redpants' shoes in the *Daily News* and tucks them under his arm.

"What're you bothering with her shoes for?" the relief man asks. "They locked her up."

"She'll be back," Bobby says. "They always come back."

Three years before, the girl was not in the least malicious. Ambitious yes, malicious no. On the all-night Greyhound from Detroit to New York she changed professions six times. Beautician, salesgirl, cocktail waitress . . . then dreaming in loftier circles . . . dancer, fashion designer, model. As a pretty black girl in 1968 she was bringing up the rear of America's consumer ethic. Her expectations derived from television commercials. And from vacuous Sidney Poitier movies and the promises after riots. If a pretty black girl puts her mind and body together and *gets down,* that is, insinuates her full powers on the unsuspecting city, here at the epicenter of a culture that celebrates killers and whores (so long as they can be exploited by the merchandisers and the media), well, Johnny, anything can happen.

"Well, Johnny, I posed for a few hosiery ads and bingo, they put me on the cover of *Cosmopolitan*."

She had rehearsed for her imaginary appearance on the Johnny Carson Show by talking back to the screen in Sammy's Rest, a highway stop through which passed many salesmen who insisted, until she believed it, that she was wasting herself as a waitress. She was twenty-six. Weary of her solitary life. Hungry for people and tinsel.

From the Port Authority building, she walked directly to Miss Dixie's Employment Agency in Times Square. A cardboard suitcase slapped against her long legs and she was feeling as reckless as a kite. They told her she could do day work.

When she came out of Miss Dixie's, he was waiting. A voluptuous figure of a man, radiantly clothed and well displayed against what looked like a metal rhinoceros (in fact it was a custom Eldorado with a Rolls-Royce front mounted with Texas steer horns). He was grinning.

"What you want to wash Whitey's floor for?"

"I'm a model, thank you." And she huffed off.

He was in the same spot the next day and the next. "How's the modeling business?" His arrogance was insufferable. She knew the type, a dope pusher most likely. Yet for a black man so young, his prosperity was impressive. Fitted in the finest vines and kicks of the day, pepper silks and Alpaca fronts and Halloween socks matched to his half-gaiters, he lounged against his metal rhinoceros without a flicker of exertion.

"Like my short?" He stroked his car, which was anything but short.

She sniffed at his street slang. It was evident that she liked his short.

Day work was out. So, very nearly, was her money.

On the fifth day, sensing there was some knack for

controlling one's destiny in this city which she did not have—and which he apparently did have, damn him —she answered his tease with a slap.

"Good!" he said. "I like my women to have spunk."

In the car with her he withdraws a fifty-dollar bill pressed under the cellophane of his cigarette pack, unrolls it, and snorts a white powder into his nose. "Like a whiff?" The girl retreats into her lavender spring coat. "Jus' a little cocaine to clear the passages. Six hundred dollars an ounce."

"I'm not a dopie. I'm a model with a daughter to support and a husband in Vietnam and I don't take to a man just 'cause he's dressed fancy," she lies, trying to negotiate a favorable self-image.

"Sugarman digs you, baby. Men are all suckers 'cause they looking to protect their glands. Women run this joint. A smart girl can make any man her bloodhound. Sugarman has nothin' but respect for a girl like you."

It takes her a while to understand that Sugarman always speaks of himself in the third person. By then the car is spinning through the East Side and he is doing his father-daughter routine. "Men have always roughed you around, right? If you was my girl I'd touch you like velvet, drink you like champagne. You could cry to Sugarman."

"I'm not interested in sex," she lies. "I need money."

He is in the modeling business himself, he says. "All the girls in my agency are white but—," he flips back her coat, "you shine like brass. Accordin' to Whitey's color scheme you'll pass, jus' fine. But you can't go out with Sugarman dressed like that!"

In the back room of an East Village boutique a small Indian man brings on a selection of exotic clothes. The girl swoons over the mirrored boleros and chooses a pair of crimson velvet pants. "I can cut the legs off when it gets hot."

"You know your assets, honey." Sugarman builds her up and up. "Legs is what a man looks for, not faces, and you got one *hellifying* pair of legs." He walks around her, mumbling. "Hey, I got you a professional name. Redpants."

"Quite so," the Indian man says.

Suddenly Sugarman fades toward the door. The Indian shopkeep is stroking her arm. With her false cockiness exposed and the pimp's seductive teeth already sinking in, the girl pleads: "Don't leave me alone."

"Redpants, you and me gonna party all night! But right now Sugarman has got to check in with the other models in his dynamite agency." And then the little whisper in her ear: *You like the man's vines? Give him a cheap giggle. Try on some more and walk around with your titties dangling.* "Me and my short will be by in an hour, honey."

The Indian was what they call an easy trick, which is how the smart street pimp eases his girls into the trade. (It also pays for the clothes.) From there he drives Redpants up Third Avenue and introduces her to the rest of his stable.

"Say hello to Horseface, she's my French import. Rotten face but a body like creampuffs." Horseface is a pubescent girl from the Canadian provinces whom Sugarman recruited in Montreal. She smiles dumbly.

"This here's Kimp. She's got four kids and she bought herself a big house in Philadelphia. I saw the deeds. Kimp, she comes to work for me and makes herself a coupla grand and stays away awhile, and comes back again. Got herself a husband now. He don't know nothin' about her professional life. But she came back to Sugarman, isn't that so?"

Kimp nods her red Marie Antoinette wig. She is about thirty-five and her face appears to be bolted over steel plates. Only one complaint from Kimp—her teen-aged sons are beginning to ask what kind of work she does up in New York. "I tell them I work for the city."

Sugarman beckons Redpants across the hall of this modern high-rise in the Murray Hill section where he keeps his girls. He pays the $350 rent; two girls share an apartment and at least one generally has a child with her. He lives in a better pad on a higher floor in the same building, for purposes of surveillance.

"Now you're gonna meet the hustlingest dame in Sugarman's agency. College girl, real class. She was a track star at this dum-dum nun's school of hers. She can outrun anybody—cars, cops, anybody 'cept Sugarman of course."

He rings. "Road Runner?"

A pair of dark eyes, painted beneath with zebra stripes, peer around the door. "Hello, you bastard. I'm busy."

A child is crying in the dimness behind Road Runner. The young woman is nude except for a Catholic medal on a chain.

"Redpants here needs employment." Sugarman spins the new girl around by the hair. "She's a model."

The eyes narrow in appraisal. How old? Is she clean? Any habit? Any experience on the street? Sugarman answers for his probationer, whose attention is wholly distracted by the apartment. Though sparsely furnished and humorless, it is, in the eyes of a girl from a rooming house in Detroit, the quintessence of glamour.

Road Runner reaches for the girl's cardboard suitcase. "I'll try her out in the Lindy tonight and see what she's got." The door shuts.

Grinning, strutting, enormously pleased with himself, Sugarman sweeps Redpants off to dinner and double Scotches at a First Avenue bar in the 70s. She notices that everyone knows him here. And that all the men wear the same hat. Whether it's Panama straw or felt, trimmed with peacock or parrot feathers, its big plate brim is tipped at a preposterous diagonal. This is the street pimp's cockscomb, the big bad dude Capone hat.

Redpants is not quite sure what she is into, but Sugarman is so kind. . . .

"We got a little family here, see?" he purrs. "You don't have to be lonely no more."

Wonderland! In the Belmont Plaza drugstore Road Runner is outfitting her with eye expanders, false lashes from Andrea's European Hair collection. She chooses Exotics Black, which are clumped like shrubs. Then a gloss of Pearl Drops toothpaste, her pick of six varieties of hair dryer, and birth control pills. Road Runner explains the pills must be taken every day of the month to obliterate any flow and its interference with business.

What's this? One whole window is devoted to a display of foot remedies, Dr. Scholl in his vast orange inventory, and on the counter, tonight's feature: For Feet's Sake refresher spray. Redpants laughs.

"Must be a lot of old folks aroun' here."

Road Runner looks at her recruit in astonishment.

"You're a working girl now. We walk!"

This is the first time Redpants confronts her position directly. She panics. Shrinking back, retreating from Road Runner, she flies into the street. Running does not help. She is still captive of her motives. Every girl on the verge of turning out must pass through this quick hell, wrestling with the urges and illusions that have brought her this far. A pimp often drugs a girl at this point. Or he has sex with her and makes her feel needed, then suggests she have a few "dates" for pay, hoping that the customers will reinforce her sense of being wanted. Or the girl herself continues to observe the life style of the prostitutes around her until she learns the value of criminal behavior and takes up the code: exploit before being exploited. For Redpants the pull was out of oblivion toward adventure. . . .

She must have belonged to somebody at one time. To the Baptist preacher who was her father (they said) *or to the vague brothers and sisters who passed through her bedroom after the preacher disappeared* (died, they said). *Or to the proud, liverish flesh of her mother, who now presides over a rooming house of alcoholics. Her mother collects cigarette butts for the men she looks after. She keeps them in a glass jar. Those half-smoked cigarettes must also have belonged to somebody at one time. But they always went bad in the jar.*

Road Runner catches up with her on Park Avenue. In strong terms she lays out the philosophy: The working girl is honest; the rest of the world is the con. Straight women exchange sex for financial security and the respected social status of marriage. You have no status, no power, and no way to get it except by using your snapper. You give it away, why? You're sitting on a gold mine! We prossies provide a product in more demand than the world's best-selling book. *Don't let life just happen to you.* Get out there and hustle for yourself!

The outlook of this once-Catholic refugee from the California suburbs is simply a direct application of American capitalism circa 1960s: fast, aggressive, confident of the growth of urban lust and prepared to indulge it, manipulate it, and cash in on it.

For reinforcement, Road Runner walks her protégée once through the Waldorf. It smells of face powder and ballroom polish, the light scents of remote sources of money.

It is late now. Across the street two fat pinky-ring Johns with Shriner's pins in their lapels step out of the Belmont Plaza. They barely have time to buy the latest copy of *Screw*. Girls whiptail from three corners like guppies fighting for the last crumb at the top of a fish tank.

"Go get him," Road Runner says. She quickly instructs Redpants on where to take a trick of this kind and how long to spend and how much to ask for.

Leading the John up the warped stairs of the Lindy Hotel, a second-floor fleabag several blocks down from the Waldorf, Redpants looks as awkward as she feels. Behind the desk is a beefy man in a mustard undershirt, his arms blue with tattoos. He smiles at Redpants by way of a welcome into the fold.

"That's $7.75, pal." The John fills out a registration card. Halfway up the staircase the couple is stopped by a shout from the tattooed man.

"Hey, you're man and wife, right?"

Redpants giggles. "Right."

Speaking as a professor to a new student, he points

to the registration card. "Well, you gotta put it down, sweetheart." Of course, his protection.

Nothing in the room but a glass night lamp on a table and, set flat out under the windows like a cheap placemat, the bed. Above it rattle curtains of plastic brocade. Fluorescence intrudes; across the street is a block of windows framing eccentric postal workers at their night labors. Fixing on those windows, she bites down on the plastic brocade curtains and gives him fifteen minutes for 30 dollars.

Redpants thus earned a position as Sugarman's new "bottom woman." To celebrate, he let her spend the night in his apartment. She did a little bit of crying and he cleared her passages with cocaine. He stroked her, gently, not rushing her, absorbing all her defenses into his fatherly possession, and released her. Then he put on his hat and went out. "There's more where that came from," he said, "but you got to prove yourself a hustler before it's yours."

Redpants learned the games of her trade very quickly.

The Badger Game: She lures a man up to a hotel room. As the pair disrobe, Sugarman bursts in taking the part of the outraged husband. She whimpers to the John that they both will be killed unless he hands over his money, which he usually does.

Variations of the Badger Game. Horseface and Kimp are waiting in the closet when Redpants enters with a trick. He pays in advance. When she has him wholly engaged, the other girls creep out and relieve his trousers of excess bills. "If he misses his bread, we'll jump him," Road Runner says. "If that doesn't work, cut him up a little."

Redpants balks at using her knife. "It's your insurance policy," the experienced hooker instructs. "These Johns are all married men. They're going to have a hard enough time explaining a few blade marks when they get home. Even if they call the cops in the heat of the moment, they are never going to get up on that stand and tell the judge they got stung by three hookers in a hotel room. It's giving the wife a gift divorce case! Another thing, never forget the stud complex. These Johns are jellyballs or they wouldn't be sniffing around chippies in the first place. They can't stand admitting women can get down and do raw deeds."

To supplement her street trade, Sugarman introduces Redpants to her first "oddball trick." He is a functionary in the Municipal Building. Twice monthly, for $50, she has only to take him home and admire the lacy lingerie concealed under his bland suit.

"Oddball tricks are where the money is," Sugarman assures her.

But when Redpants turns up an oddball of her own, the pimp is not so encouraging. The TV personality with a kiddie show says he wants a boy, while Redpants and Road Runner watch. He is ready to write a thousand-dollar check. She can't find a homosexual to save herself. Sugarman is jowling with his friends at Tommy Small's bar when Redpants bursts in with her demand.

"I ain't no faggot!" shouts the insulted pimp.

"As of now, sugar, you is."

Redpants knew that the fast girls worked the Waldorf. She soon learned the routine.

When show biz or sports celebrities or their friends check into their suites in the Waldorf Towers, they pass the word to the guards on the door: do not stop any of the girls.

So, near dawn on the day before a pivotal boxing match at Madison Square Garden, Redpants breezed past Bobby the Guard and said confidently, "I'm going up to see the king."

"You must be kidding," Bobby said, knowing of the boxer's puritanical bent. Bobby allowed the girl into the lobby to use the house phone. The boxer came down bellowing; Bobby apologized. The beautiful chippie in red velvet pants swept off with the boxer in the Towers elevator and thus became—for better or for worse—a Waldorf girl.

For Christmas Sugarman gave all his hookers stolen mink scarfs. And two nights off.

It gets in the blood. All night long peeping and hiding, zipping and lacing. Hustling bucks and ducking the Third Division boys, those earnest young plainclothesmen assigned to the vice squad who work out of the 17th Precinct on the East Side. The pace itself, the sheer velocity of risk, is a drug. And then a girl *controls* the situation with her tricks. (Not so in allied fields such as modeling and acting, Sugarman points out correctly.) She sets the price and delivers the pleasure, or doesn't, pretending submission while all the time she is in control. Can it be sensed by anyone straight, the exhilaration of a young street hooker? If she is fast, and Redpants is very very fast, the payoff can never be duplicated. It gets in the blood like gambler's fever.

Gucci shoes. Double Scotches. Kanekalon wigs in a kaleidoscope of colors. Ten-dollar tips to the Belmont Plaza bartenders, fifteen to the Barclay doormen, a fifty-dollar bill for Bobby the Guard tossed with a winner's smile—she always had a smile for Bobby. "I'm making four and five hundred a night," Redpants announced. "That's a dollar a minute!" She selected her men now, circling the Waldorf with her impudent hips controlled like a jib sail and nodding only to businessmen in well-cut suits.

After a year on the Street Sugarman was allowing her 5 percent. Her money came and went like liquid fuel. Near dawn she would squander the last on a crippled newsboy or a bum, as if to ward off a similar fate. How is a prostitute to open a savings account? What does she tell the IRS? Most street pimps collect the full night's take and simply *manage* the financial affairs of the stable. That is, for two to six girls a pimp buys hot clothes, pays the rent and doctor bills, and shows up in court to pay the fines. All his girls call him husband. He calls his favorite "wife" and the rest of his stable settle for the status of "wife-in-laws." Generally speaking, as a social unit, they all get on very well.

Only Bobby watched as would a father, with a sense of foreboding. Redpants was drinking too hard, spending too recklessly, running too fast.

"Save your money, little girl, don't be throwin' these tips around."

Redpants squeezed his hand. "You can't live in this world by yourself."

And then they busted Sugarman and the trouble began.

The pimp had suggested Redpants phone her girl friend in Detroit. "Tell her you're living high off a Park Avenue family and you have her a job as a nanny too." He sent the plane fare.

They met the girl friend at La Guardia: Redpants, Sugarman, and his metal rhinoceros with the introductory envelope of cocaine. "We got a little family here . . ." The new girl protested. In Road Runner's apartment she was dressed up and slapped around and, in a numb terror, sent out on the street. In two hours, unbeknown to her procurers, the new girl was picked up in a general pross bust.

The story spilled out in the bullpen at the Criminal Courthouse on Centre Street where the girl confided it to a policewoman. Accompanied by two plain-clothesmen, she returned to Road Runner's apartment and whined for Sugarman to let her in only three hours after he had put her on the street.

"You goddam worthless broad—" He lunged for the girl with a kitchen knife and then he went downtown with the police. Hoping for the nearly impossible, a Third Division lieutenant charged the pimp with compulsory prostitution and coaxed the girl to testify. Almost never does a prostitute testify against her pimp. She was placed in a midtown hotel with a police-woman at the door. Hearings came and went with the usual time-killing postponements.

"Let's be scuffling," Road Runner said, having been left in charge of the business.

The pimp's bail was deliberately prohibitive, $5,000, and Redpants could no longer afford to be choosy. Three kinds of tricks the Waldorf Girls routinely scorn are nonwhites, boys without ties, and drunks. By the end of the month Redpants had been through all of them except a black boy.

"What're you doing out here buying pussy dressed like that?" she scolds the boy in UFO jeans. He is a handsome dude with the Harlem in him half buried under a prep school accent.

"Are you waiting for anyone?" he says shyly.

"Maybe."

"We could blow some grass at my place—"

"I'm no dopie. What're you, a cop?"

He turns slowly while she fingers his sides and back.
"I'm not too good at patting; sure you don't have a
piece [gun]?" Her voice is soft and wishful. Redpants' reaction to the absence of Sugarman, and to the
lost sense of belonging, is an indiscriminate need to in-
gratiate herself with everyone: counter men, cabbies,
cops. She has even turned for sexual comfort to Road
Runner. Collectively, these peripheral contacts will
add up at day's end to all the love coming in.

The boy is kind. Uptown in his cramped bedroom
he plays her Jimi Hendrix records and lets her cry and
finally offers her some wood. "Wood?" Like oil in an
overheated engine, the heroin makes her feel better,
smoother, and then she stops feeling at all.

"These days you don't know who to trust," Sugarman says. Redpants and Road Runner and her baby
are curled up together like spaniel pups, watching TV,
when he springs through their apartment door. "Isn't
that the truth?"

The girls say it's the truth all right, except for their
own little family. They bring him chocolate milk and
a joint. He does not bother to explain that the frightened witness split for Detroit and without her the
police case against him collapsed.

"Our little family." Sugarman smiles, but his mouth
hangs away from his teeth like a dog's who cannot be
said for certain to be playing. "Funny, I heard somebody put a bad mouth on me."

His girls look blank.

"Also heard Redpants went down with a nigger
cop."

"He was no cop!"

"Hey, Sugarman's a racist." Road Runner laughs and begins dancing about the room to cheer him up.

"Got anything in your titty bank for Sugarman?"

Road Runner assures him she gave all her money to the pimp designated to bail him out.

"That's funny—'cause Sugarman heard you was holdin' out." He dives at the dancing girl and snatches off her brassiere, and a snow of small bills flutters to the floor.

Whimpering like puppies who cannot hope to convince an irate master of their innocence, but who cannot sleep without his stroke . . . *We scuffled for you, Sugarman* . . . they follow him to the closet where he selects a wooden hanger . . . *You're our man for all time, Sugarman* . . . and into the bathroom where he wraps the hanger with absorbent cotton. Redpants kisses the back of his neck. The pimp whirls and thrashes both girls until their bodies lie like rag dolls on the bathroom floor. Then he removes the cotton and mops his brow with it, satisfied that the hanger left no bruises to interfere with his source of income.

Speed, mobility, and numbers—Sugarman enumerates the advantages of their new game. His girls will rent a car. They park on a side street close to Lex in a Grand Prix. A man stops for the Don't Walk sign. When two pretty girls wave he is flattered; the door swings wide and he slides in between them. They drive toward the river and park. While one girl toys with him, the other lifts his wallet, removes the cash and credit cards, and returns the wallet. Neat, sporting. Unless the John is a jumpy type, in which case the girls may be required to slug, bite, or knife him and leave the remains on the street.

So went the successful summer of 1970. Sugarman

and his friends sat in a Lexington Avenue bar tapping their high-heeled shoes. The girls knew their quotas: $250 a night each. They also knew their man was never more than six blocks away; the bar is close to the Waldorf and has local sports on cable TV. Each night the Joint Chiefs of the Peacock gathered to admire themselves there. *Love* that summer uniform— the tank-top jumpsuit s-t-r-e-t-c-h-e-d like taffy over the chocolate net, see-through, pectoralis major body shirt. Somewhere on the ensemble there are nailheads. Admire them too. And the big bad dude Capone hat. This is a business of externals, after all. The Pimp Style screams heavy bucks and lazy power. On the street it carries all the status of the dope dealer without the dangers. In fact the Pimp Style is becoming so popular that one can scarcely distinguish a genuine working pimp from the pimp poseurs who hang out at Le Drugstore, and the two-bit Queens teenies in high-heeled Florsheims who *aren't even black* but who have discovered that the corner of Lex and 49th is the new freak showcase.

This is the beauty of street pimping. The men provide no customers. They run almost no risk of arrest. Consequently, while their hookers are hustling against a 4:00 A.M. deadline, there is absolutely nothing for the pimps to do. They watch cable TV in the nearest bar.

The tall Road Runner, pale and liquid as skimmed milk, and the long-legged Redpants, with her gleaming brass skin, make a stunning pair. Their fortunes are assured, except for one thing. Nobody likes a pushy hooker.

"Those two are taking the trade away from all us old-timers and bringing down the cops," Dutchman complains to Bobby the Guard. Bobby says it isn't the

girls but their pimp. If they had any sense they would
cut him loose. But Road Runner in particular has gone
greedy and vicious. She is not getting any younger. As
she says, "I know the winners are out there, and this
is my ninth race."

Fall went cold early. The normal hoarding instinct
on the street became more desperate, owing to the
competition, and now the older girls put the cops on
Road Runner and Redpants. Arrests soared. Their
lawyer wanted $250 a case. Their records grew fat
as composition books, and because they had to plead
guilty to stay out of the cage, the fines began to hurt.
In less than two months the girls who drove the Grand
Prix spent $10,000 on court fines and payoffs.

The Queen of the Pickpockets saw her chance to
break them. Word was around about a pack of West
Side girls who specialized in robbing hookers. She
found them and made a deal. After midnight on a list-
less Friday on Lex, the old crone gave the nod. The
West Side pack crept up on the Grand Prix. They
muzzled Road Runner and Redpants, commandeered
their car, and drove them to the river. When the two
girls came back it was on foot with long grape-colored
fingernail tracks all over their bodies.

"I've seen them before, on Broadway," Kimp remembered. "Big Texas girls." Road Runner would not
speak. She led Redpants across town to the Mobil
station under the West Side Highway and bought a
Coke and washed them off with it. Then they hunted
Times Square for five girls in a Grand Prix. On 44th
Street they passed a group of stumbledrunk boys.

"C'meer, you dirty whore," a boy in combat boots
said.

Road Runner told him to get lost and kept walking. She still had the Coke bottle.

"Lemme have your dirty whore sister then."

Suddenly Redpants began to laugh, at herself, at her humorless white partner with the Catholic medal around her bleeding neck, at the whole bleeding shell game which this night, in one night, they had lost. "Cut the crap," Road Runner said. More laughter, and now the drunk boys joined in. Road Runner walked over to a mailbox and broke the glass bottle against it and then she walked back to the boy in combat boots and drove the bottle into the soft place above his collarbone. The next morning she left for California.

"Why don't you go home, honey?" Bobby the Guard urges Redpants; she had been walking the street all night Saturday and all night Sunday. "You know weekends is dead out there."

She shakes her head. Sugarman does not yet know about Road Runner, the robbery, the car, and she is not about to go home until she has something to show. Her head throbs. Where the Coke has dried on her scratches the itching is cruel.

Near dawn she congratulates herself on her perseverance. A balding gentleman steps out of the Waldorf for his morning constitutional. Agreed: she will knock on his door, room 3700, at seven o'clock. At this point Redpants is not in a position to negotiate price, nor would she jeopardize Bobby the Guard, looking the way she does, by using the elevator. She runs up all thirty-seven flights of service stairs.

"You cheap baldassed degenerate little bastard!"

Babbling and weeping and running again, down all 37 flights of service stairs, down 444 cement steps, the girl in torn red pants emerges on the marble landing of Bobby the Guard's lobby—*he offered me ten dollars*—and passes out at his feet.

Wan morning light. Rattle of plastic brocade curtains. Bobby's words blow around the hotel room for which she insisted on paying ($7.75 out of her last $10) and where she waited for him because she needed a man. Bobby is talking:

"Get out of this racket while you still can, honey. It gets in your blood, this gamblin' game. It deals women hard. I seen a lotta girls, they say they won't be out here but a year. They goin' to secretarial school durin' the day or they got a house to remodel. Once in a while they gets out in time. Most of 'em gets hooked. You're a beautiful girl, Redpants, but you're beginnin' to go. Look at these tracks in your arms—they givin' you the needle now too?"

Bobby's voice drifts through her fever. Nothing holds. A limpness in her belly tells her she needs an abortion; she doesn't want to think about that. She needs money, that's all. She could buy a house in Philly like Kimp and live there with Sugarman and when the bread was down she could come back and hook a while, but nothing holds. Bobby holds her hands and talks. All those murdered nights compress in her ears and whine, *you came so close,* but she doesn't want to think about that back here in the Lindy Hotel.

"I'd better be movin' now. With Road Runner gone, Sugarman will be counting on me."

"That beat artist? He's got himself a home in Westchester and now they tell me he's in the taxi business. That's right, 'bout to buy his second gypsy cab."

Redpants refuses to take this information into her mind. "He's all the family I got left." She strokes Bobby's gentle, wretched face. "And you." Abruptly her mood shifts. "Ten dollars. I should have given that baldie a busted head!"

Bobby gives her the look that all through the ages men have given prostitutes whom they dreamed of redeeming. It is part guilt, part naïveté, part male fantasy. She chins up on that look, rising to her full height and striking a pose by the door. "Did you know I was a model?"

Redpants leaves Bobby at the corner of the Waldorf. The Queen of the Pickpockets is across the street, waving.

"Sugarman has a mind to sell you, Redpants."

"Sell?"

"To put on his cab. He's got you sold for two hundred dollars."

That made it easy. As of now Redpants would be an independent.

Winter is a bad game. Redpants drifts westward to hook on the White Way. Later at night, deeper into winter, she finds herself drawn to Eighth Avenue. In 1970 this was the land of gold teeth and wood fiends— junkie hookers who hit the downside of the hill at thirty and were clinging to heroin to break the fall a while. The very old ones are known as petrified wood. They will gladly sell their favors for a five-dollar bag.

Wood keeps a girl warm, but the sense of time goes and her performance becomes sloppy. Redpants keeps moving.

Ninth Avenue is a desolate street; essentially it is an approach to the Lincoln Tunnel. Toward the end of the Sixties, a wholly new and virulent subculture of prostitution attached itself to all those dim intersections and took hold. *The contagion along Ninth Avenue,* Deputy Inspector Irving Roth of the 14th Precinct called it. "We have a unique problem with those prostitutes," he said. "They engage in what they consider the proper act of prostitution, except that physically they are males."

"They faggots over there?" Redpants asks a six-foot white female impersonator one night. He shakes his blond wig. "Some yes, some no. Most of us is just working a good gig. We stop the truck drivers heading for New Jersey and do them in the truck or do them in a hallway. All you got to say is 'It's my time of the month, honey, but I'll make it up to you.'"

"What happens when the policewoman searches you?"

"She gives a screech."

Redpants laughs at this con of cons. To kill time, for there is no apartment now in which to sleep, she walks over to Tenth to see for herself. So this is the next rung down in her westward drift. The bottom. Frail, pathetic men with white boots laced over their shaven calves, toiling in erotic chaos. The parody is grotesque. How dare these sexual gargoyles distort the best of what she has been? She runs. Pulling together her old airs and graces, she hails a taxi. "Lexington Avenue, please."

Every night thereafter she finished up the necessary business on Broadway and taxied back to the East Side at scavenger hour, after four, to work the Waldorf. Her bedroom became Grand Central Station.

Can't see my legs anymore. Why don't they put a full-length mirror in this washroom? Mean place. Mean little sinks. Tip Here soap. Don't like washing a nice dress here, the red runs in the rotten soap. Scales don't work. Ankles swelling, a girl don't need a scale to know when her ankles are swole up like grapefruits.

Got to cut down on the wood. Winter's a bummer. Be nice to be busted and get a little rest where it's warm. Hold on, girl! Spring is convention season. Come spring you can sleep in that pretty little park next to St. Bartholomew's Church.

Such are the pressures of pride and conventional morality on the hooker: Redpants would not sleep in the public waiting room. She hung around the train platforms, pretending to wait for her husband. When the GE Housewares Servicenter opened, she stood outside the glass window and studied the wives with their utilitarian haircuts, frowning over their toasters, secure in their discharge of the thousand details of domestic routine. Would she be happy? Could she fake it and forget the Life? But thinking of the future was not something Redpants liked to do.

The Gucci shoes caught his eyes. Extended stiff out from between two tall metal lockers, on the lower level near his subway, they caused Bobby the Guard to shudder. He pressed two fingers against the swollen ankle. A pulse, thank God. Deep in the slot between two lockers, slumped on a camp stool, Redpants was only asleep. He tucked a twenty-dollar bill under the arch of her foot.

GERMANY'S STRAUSS MUGGED BY 3 V-GIRLS

Spring 1971 came in with a bang for the hooking business, and its clients. Celebrities and foreign dignitaries were suffering the ignominious brutalities that formerly had been practiced only on toy salesmen and recalcitrant bookkeepers and had thus passed unreported. Now a spokesman for the police commissioner assures the public that extra details of undercover men have been assigned to "the problem of prostitutes harassing tourists, businessmen and commuters." Mayor Lindsay expresses his deep concern to Franz Josef Strauss, the prominent West German political leader whose picture was all over the newspapers. . . .

> He was returning to the Plaza shortly after 2:30 A.M. when a yellow car pulled up . . . before the 51-year-old Strauss knew what happened he was being dragged into the car . . . the three girls pulled and pushed and the big husky German found himself on the sidewalk flat on his back. Two suspects were captured and police reported that they recovered $80 in German currency. [*New York Daily News*, March 16]

Redpants is waiting her turn in Manhattan Supreme Court when Judge Culkin calls the suspects.

"Okay, Phillips and Gonzales."

Gonzales, dark-skinned and wearing a chalky blond wig, swings an ample heft up the aisle. Phillips is tall, white, and blotchy with spaces between her teeth.

"Bulldykes," whispers a knowledgeable pimp.

The judge raises their bail to $5,000 each. Somebody pays and the case is indefinitely postponed and the two suspects vanish before Redpants is done laughing. Her own case is conditionally discharged. And then the old fraternity of pross lawyers, pimps, and street girls gathers in the hall to gossip.

"Grand Central is where it's happening," declares a pimp. "I see some afflooooent muthabusinessmen picking up these daytime broads."

"Commuters don't like to shop around," explains a lawyer who is in court today to defend an engineer on a rare John collar. "You'll see them walk into the station, wait five minutes to duck their bridge partners, then they pop across the street and into a taxi with their regular hookups."

Redpants is intrigued.

"But this one, she's the duchess of the Waldorf." Her old lawyer squeezes Redpants' arm affectionately. "Where've you been?"

A bondsman from New Jersey says he saw the girl on Ninth Avenue, hanging around the tunnel approaches.

"Not Redpants!" she sniffs, for she too has taken to referring to herself in the third person. In a voice haughty with the scorn of a former Waldorf girl, she says, "On Ninth Avenue they do it in the *halls*."

Grinning, strutting, enormously pleased with her new red leatherette hot pants (the bondsman has staked her), the experienced hooker takes up her new position across from Grand Central. What could these bourgeois housewives from Long Island know about pleasing a man?

Mr. Sample has a limousine.

"How about a little drink? At my place?"

Redpants trails a finger all around Mr. Sample's limousine and over the official City of New York emblem. "I only drink at the Waldorf," she says, and she tosses off.

The limousine laps at the curb in line with Redpants' aimless path down Park Avenue. "For you, I go to the Waldorf," Mr. Sample says.

Bobby the Guard is laughing so hard he doesn't know if he's crying or what. Redpants drinking Pink Ladies again in the Bull and Bear! This little district judge is crazy about her; he won't let her go.

"And so you'll wait for my chauffeur?" the man croons in the lobby as the girl in red pants backs to-

ward the door. "Tomorrow in the same spot?" Mr.
Sample's hands grope desperately for his billfold because they have been playing this argument all night
and he is not winning.

"If you see me, you see me." She tosses the bill to
Bobby, smiling.

The poker-faced chauffeur catches up with Redpants
outside Liggett's the next afternoon. He extends a card
through the window. "Mr. Sample's Bonwit Teller
charge card. I'm to drop you off to buy a beach wardrobe."

The girl puzzles. "Beach?"

"Mr. Sample has a beach house in East Hampton,"
the chauffeur adds, icily snobbish as are most atten-
dants of the rich. "He will join you for the weekend."

No trace of Redpants on the street for two weeks.
The grapevine assumed the obvious. "She must have
taken the wrong needle." Bobby the Guard cursed
himself; he should have known when she threw him
the bill that Redpants was not in her right state of
mind.

*Sitting . . . all day sitting in a richbitch bathtub, sit-
ting on a taffeta couch . . . watching color TV with a
Costa Rican maid . . . ain't it a game? a whole maid
hired to guard Redpants . . . nothing to do but sit in
sun rooms with a maid who can't speak English and
wait for Mr. Sample to bring home the cocaine . . . all
powdered up under Pucci-poo titty pink pye-jamas . . .
living jus' like the TV commercials . . .*

Close to midnight one Friday she comes lollygag-
ging down Lexington in long silky beach pajamas, one
tiny white stone pinned like a star on each ear.

"Redpants, we thought you was dead!"

"Near to it," she says. "Can you imagine me sitting in a tub all day, waiting for a dirty old man?"

Bobby the Guard says some girls would think that was just fine.

"Not Redpants," she says. "I'd rather be out here peepin' and hustlin' and duckin' the cops. It's what I know."

A siren licks down the avenue outside the brass-trimmed door. The girl in beach pajamas bristles. She yanks up her hem and kicks off her Guccis and then she is gone.

Her words come back.

"Hold my shoes!"

Chapter Three

Times Square was about to throw a final fatal
clot. Its major vessels had been clogging with
prostitutes, criminals and fear. From spring
to fall of 1972 the cops stepped up their
game of tag with the hookers, while certain
middle fish grew richer and cockier, bringing
into open combat ...

DELLA BELLA
AND THE PROSS VAN

The best view of the game is beside Jimmy Della Bella—*Jimmy of the beautiful*—who operates the two bus-
iest prostitution hotels on Eighth Avenue. Barebacked,
toes curled, he crouches for hours like a baby gorilla
at the second-floor window of the Hotel Raymona,
watching for police cars and prostitution vans.
Mounted on the sill is a reflector that points toward
Broadway and mirrors the oncoming traffic. Just inside the window is a portable TV. Jimmy Della Bella
spends his days in a rotted swivel chair, shifting his
eyes back and forth between the Cyclopean reflector
and the Fischer-Spassky match on TV. He is also a
chess fan.

In the reflector the playing field looks like a giant fish
tank. A shark has entered the waters: the "pross" van.

"Get baaaaaaaaaaaaaaaaaack!" he shouts.

A quiver runs through the jellyfish Johns lined up across the street. Like minnows the girls below the window gather into an unnatural school and flush back into the long dark hall of the hotel. It smells of urine and milkshakes. This hall is where the girls wait between tricks, displaying their torsos through the windowed door and sucking on Mr. Custards and waiting for the buzzer to sound, permitting the Johns to come in from the street. Only when the street is clean of cops does Jimmy release the door from upstairs. Up to seventy-five girls a day work out of the Raymona. Each one uses a bed eight to ten times. Each time the John donates $20 to her and $10 to the hotel. It is therefore in the interest of Jimmy Della Bella to keep the game moving. He hoists himself atop the window sill and the very instant the tail of the squad car disappears around the corner, he shouts to the girls again:

"Okaaaaaaaaaaaaaaaaaaay!"

Girls plunge back into the street.

The Raymona is situated in the heart of Hell's Bedroom on the corner of 49th Street and Eighth Avenue. It has thirty-two rooms, twelve of them home to gummy old men, four of whom are friendless welfare drunks, two of whom have been rotting here since 1947. (The days when it was home to Kirk Douglas and Burt Lancaster are long gone.) The five rooms on the second floor are the ones used for "illicit sexual congress." Between January 1971 and June 1972 the Raymona scored eighty-eight arrests and thirty-three convictions for the misdemeanors of prostitution or permitting prostitution—well above the score of any other midtown fleabag—not to mention the incessant roundups for loitering.

Tonight, Friday, August 11, the Raymona is running lucky. Only one pross collar will be made in the hallway. (The previous week police busted Cindy Sadd, Yvette Carlson and John Masterson all in one evening.) A low fog of filth lies over all surfaces, which in lieu of being cleaned are covered with towels. The office is small but homey: a beat-up cabbage-rose rug, a copy of the *Daily Racing Form,* an old man's hat and cane hung on the door. Dad and Mom Della Bella are down visiting today. Homey. The old man is a retired bookmaker from Waterbury. Now young Phil Della Bella comes steaming up the stairs. He can be distinguished from his weedy-haired brother by lamb chop sideburns and a USMC tattoo.

"It's okay. I seen the cop turn up Fiftieth."

Jimmy Della Bella lights a Kool and sits back in the path of a groaning fan. "Like I say, this is the usual August harassment. It'll break, end of September."

Has he seen anyone go out of business since the mayor's crackdown on midtown prostitution?

"Nah. Who are they hurtin'? If the girls aren't here, they're in the Waldorf-Astoria." He touches the last two words with respect. Della Bella is a small fish. The first time I met him he was handcuffed to a school desk in the Midtown North station house for obstructing a pross arrest in his hotel. But he has been playing the game a long time. Seven years ago he was a dishwasher in Queens. A Legal Aid lawyer he happened to meet in Criminal Court gave him a tip: there is a lot of green in the prostitution-hotel business. Last spring, with the profits from managing the Raymona, he took over the lease on the Hotel Lark. Today Jimmy Della Bella can afford to be philosophical. He is confident, cocky to a fault, he wants to straighten me out on a few points.

"What comes, comes. I made enough money. I'll never have to worry. They know I run this place and I hold the lease on the Lark but they can't ever connect me with it. All they know is the corporation name. It's the same corporation that owns most of the pross hotels in midtown. My name's not even on the incorporation papers."

How much money does he make, this former dishwasher with five children?

"Hey, I just built a nine-room house in the suburbs. You make $20,000 or $200,000, what's the difference?"

Roughly $180,000, I say.

"Let's don't talk dollars and cents. Do you make money or don't you make money? That's what the thing boils down to."

Prostitution arrests are a way of life around the Raymona. The monsignor of St. Malachy's, the "Actors' Church" next door, has vowed to defeat the wages of sin. But Della Bella claims to run a clean house. "Like I said to you the day you was up the precinct, you may see a lot of busts for prostitution in my places, but you won't see any complaints for robbery, burglary, mugging. You check, because there are none." I did check and there were none.

Suppose one of the girls does get out of line, I ask Della Bella.

"Don't let them in."

Can he keep them out?

"I keep all the colored out."

Isn't that racist?

"The colored are the ones that rob and cut, that's all I know."

The only dark face on the premises belongs to a crippled janitor. He has graduated several times from

Sing Sing and is happy now just buying cigars for Mr. Jimmy. The walking dead and welfare drunks who occupy the upstairs rooms seem to like it here too. There's always a little action with the girls around. Della Bella still charges the men from $15 to $25 a week, cashes their welfare checks, and takes up a daily collection for the horses at Aqueduct. Homey.

As if on cue, a shifty-looking hooker emerges from a working room and passes the office.

"Stay out of the Lark," Jimmy warns her. "I'm gonna call Steve up right now."

Steve is a clerk at the Lark Hotel, another Della Bella enterprise one block uptown from the Raymona, on Eighth Avenue. Della Bella doesn't want this girl robbing Johns on his turf.

"Hey, you wanna go in the room with a girl and see what the hell it's all about?" Della Bella offers to take me over to the Lark. He slips on Gucci loafers and a silky St. Laurent shirt.

"Watch the window, Phil."

His brother springs into action.

"Get baaaaaaaaaaaaaaaack!"

I can't see anything in the reflector but empty street.

"Squad car," Phil announces triumphantly. "Spotted him way up at the corner. See, I got very special eyes. I can see reflections in the Eugene O'Neill Theater."

From the towel-draped sink which serves as his silent butler, Della Bella picks up the prosperous pross-hotelkeeper's effects—a ring of keys, a club sandwich of tens and twenties, and a House of Windsor cigar. But before we can leave, Phil lunges across the window sill and outdoes his brother. Balanced spread-eagle on his belly like a performing seal, he peers around the corner, flicks a cigar ash with his diamond-circled pinky, and losing less than a minute's worth of play, hollers down to the girls, "Okaaaaaaaaaaaay!"

Outside, Hell's Bedroom is filling with bodies. An improbable creature bounces past us wearing white knee stockings, black patents, a pleated skirt, and a tiny white cardigan. Her hair is in pigtails.

"How ya doin'?" she calls in passing.

"Hey Valerie."

The photographer with me pouts. "When are we going to see one of your prostitutes?"

"You're looking at her."

The photographer swears all he can see is some square little kid who must be sight-seeing from the Midwest. In fact, Valerie is a nineteen-year-old former junkie who was deported at the age of thirteen for smuggling heroin out of Canada. Last year, in recognition of her brilliant career in armed robbery and dope pushing, she made the Virginia State Penitentiary. Her daughter was placed with a welfare family and Valerie decided that "tricking," though less money, was less dangerous. She is good at it. Plump, moist, wiggly, she has the appeal of a perpetually lactating spaniel.

"Why the disguise?" I asked her.

"You like my little-girl look?" Valerie says she will try anything to duck the cops. Last week she was picked up five nights out of six.

The Lark is an identical twin to the Raymona except that its Woolworth's art is of a different period. At the top of the stairs one is greeted by Gainsborough's *Blue Boy*. A shout follows us up from the street: "Anyone up there need rubbers?"

Snickers from the four girls clustered around the desk. Evidently everyone is prepared. Star player of the Lark team is a rawboned girl who is partial to pink suede boots; some call her Suede. Most working girls take so many aliases they have forgotten their real names. On the arrest forms they appear as Twinky Bizi, Cindy Sadd and other such cloying fake names. Before the judge they enjoy inventing more defiant identities: Angela Davis, Pussy La Gore, Victoria Regina.

This country supports between 200,000 and 250,000 prostitutes, more than any other nation in the Western world. To a Chinese they probably all look alike: floating mouths and disembodied hands that promise release without exacting emotion, consumers of the desperate semen backed up inside society's castoffs. In short, they are in the unidentified body prints left on the sheets after 10 million different acts of prostitution every week in America.

Della Bella suggests I slip my tape recorder under the bed of room 3. Suede lopes upstairs with her first trick. She signs the register. He peels off $10 for the room. A sign over the desk states the management is not responsible for valuables. The clerk hands her a towel. The preliminaries are always the same, as mute and dull as preparing for the dentist's chair.

The minute Suede closes the door, her trick's shoes hit the floor.

SHE: You have to pay me first, okay?
HE: I have to pay you now? Got any change?
SHE: No change.
HE: This okay?
SHE: Okay.

Through the open window the frantic loneliness of Times Square plays back . . . gears stripping, kids yelling, the long hot scream of a police siren. Into this anonymous pit they climb—a fumbling, frightened, pathetic man and a cold, contemptuous, violated woman—prepared to exchange for twenty dollars no more than ten minutes of animal sex, untouched by a stroke of their common humanity.

She doesn't even undress. She unzips.

SHE: Relax. If you're so worried about your money, honey, you can lay your head on your pants. What'll it be? Half and half?

HE: Yeah. (*he moans.*)

SHE: No kissy kissy . . .

SHE *(continuing, a few moments later):* When you have sex you have to use this.

HE: No!

SHE: Take your hand away now.

HE: Why?

SHE: You know you *have* to use this, honey, I cannot have sex with you unless you use this.

HE: I want my money back

SHE: You can't get your money back.

HE: Why?

SHE: Can't that's all. What if I have a disease?

HE: *(defensively):* Who?

SHE: You wanna catch a disease?

HE: I don't want it.

SHE: You know, people can have diseases.

HE: I want *you*.

SHE: Noooo, no no no. Not for no twenty dollars.

HE: I just want to—

SHE: *We don't do all that!*

The John gives one final anguished libidinous yowl: "I waaaaaaaaaant—" There is motion for less than a minute. "Okay?" She opens the door, slaps on her shoes, scuffs down the hall with her hot pants open and into the toilet with a contemptuous SLAM! Now she's out, washed, zipped, and darting down the stairs to catch the next trick. Time elapsed: eight minutes. Before the hour is out, Suede turns four tricks. Through it all her face remains vacant as a potato.

Business is booming in the hall. A blonde on the pay phone is making dates with her steadies. On the back of an envelope another girl has figured her week: $240, $300, $280, $200, $500. Not bad for the peak of the mayor's crackdown on prostitution. Twinky Bizi takes room 5. Two synthetic wigs sit frying on the window sill. (Most white girls have given up wearing wigs: Johns learned to look there first if they wanted their money back. So now they park cash with the clerk.) Valerie with her little-girl disguise has caught a stuttering laborer. She dispatches him and stops by Della Bella, putting him on with an impish smile: "I quit," she says.

"Take it easy," Della Bella says.

"I gotta make that two [$200] for my man. It's got so bad, he says if I don't bring in the money to-night I'll have to keep working days *and* nights. But I don't blame him," she suddenly purrs, "the man's got a lot of understanding."

Jimmy says not to worry, it's turning cold outside.

"If it gets cold, that's cool, but right now it's hot on that street." Valerie seizes the opportunity to harangue the hotelkeeper about current working conditions, a luxury never exercised with one's pimp. "Last week I worked just days, I'd be on the street at one. By six I'd have only a hundred. I'd have to hustle like crazy to make the second bill before they picked me up. I'd always call my man at ten but I'd have to say 'All I got is $140.' He'd tell me to stay out till I made my quota if it took till six in the morning! Well, five nights out of six the van took me in before ten thirty. I'd have to spend the night in the precinct, wait till noon to get out of court, and I'd have to be back out working by one P.M. I never get any sleep!"

Valerie and I walk outside together. She says goodbye, time to hustle, and is swallowed instantly in the competitive night. Now a flat-chested child appears behind the windowed door of the Lark. I wait to see what kind of trick she will catch. Eventually a bald fireplug of a man stops to negotiate; they agree to meet later.

Was he a typical-looking John? I ask the flat-chested child.

"Him? You know, he just walked away and I couldn't tell you a thing about him. They all look alike to me."

Hell's Bedroom has a thousand faces. This is the chief fact about a streetwalker's life. Every night she talks to a hundred potential customers. She has copfaces and plainclothesfaces to memorize, judgefaces to remember how to play, prossfaces to compete with, meddling pimpfaces to avoid. In one week a thousand different faces bear directly on her life. For women it is the nearest thing to war. As in the game of war, all grasp of individual human dignity eventually slips away and all others blur into one common undistinguished face: the enemy.

Five million people cross Hell's Bedroom every day. It was formerly called the 18th Precinct, a predictable sewer that carried a reputation as the nation's leading district in reported crime. Recently its boundaries were extended and now it is called Midtown North. The territory is 43rd to 59th streets, Lexington Avenue clear

west to the Hudson River. The heaviest concentration
of prostitution activity has shifted west to Eighth Avenue, from 49th to 51st streets, right across from the
hotels—safe, convenient. The crossbeam of Hell's
Bedroom is 49th Street, and that is where it begins.

Shortly before six the pimps parade their strings for
all to admire. Coming attractions: long-maned Polish
fillies from Minneapolis . . . juiced-up Southern buds
pale as magnolia petals with a kick of cocaine . . .
Marion the Librarian, so sober, could one guess she has
an arrest sheet longer than one's arm? Pimps like Fast
Black and King George don't walk down Broadway,
they *eddy*. At one time Fast Black had over twenty
girls, the biggest string on the street. Last summer the
game turned rough. Even the kingpins are down to a
couple of women. But the pimps and prossies of Hell's
Bedroom work back to back with the stars after all,
and a pro never shows strain. And so, before dusk, the
pimps slip into the labial leather orifices of their El-
dorados and sail off center-stage, proud insouciant
black swans.

The last pross van to Night Court leaves the precinct
at seven. Any girl who misses it stays in action for the
next twelve hours. In action if she's lucky, sleeping
in the precinct if she's not.

The code on the street is simple: survival of the
fastest. The police are genuine competition but rather
sporting, as a rule. Cops who ride the vans are in this
game year after year, just like the pross. Faces grow
familiar. The girls give the cops fond nicknames like
Muscles and Lurch and McGillah the Gorilla; the
cops give the sporting girls a break now and then—"If
you have any dope or weapons, get rid of them before
we get to the precinct." A loose system of ethics operates among these experienced players. Serious work-

ing girls, for instance, refer respectfully to one another as "dedicated women." They work the street from six to twelve hours a day, seven days a week, every week of winter as well as summer. Midtown North alone has twelve hundred such hard-core working girls. When the heat is on they may be pushed up, down, or across town temporarily, but they always come back to the territory where their first pimp turned them out. Which is why the dedicated women survive every cleanup.

The tie that binds is more than sentimental. Like any good salesperson, a working girl wants to be where her steady customers can find her. Even then it takes a long while to learn a territory, its faces and places, its cops and plainclothes. On strange turf a slipup is almost inevitable, as three West Side prossies discovered in August. On the spur of the moment they decided to scan the East Side for a possible move. . . .

"We had our stories down pat," they told me. "One was a model, one was a clerk. I worked for the phone company. So we get in a cab and step out on Lexington. We no sooner put our foot on the corner of Fifty-first and here comes an officer from the Seventeenth."

"He says, 'Guess what, girls? You're going in for loitering.'

"We say, 'What are you talking about? We don't even come from here!' He asks for identification. I showed him my Minneapolis driver's license. The other girls didn't have any I.D. so I said I'd just met them and I wanted to take them to a nightclub over here, the Hippydrome or something like that."

(Her fatal mistake was unfamiliarity with the neighborhood; the name of the club is the Hippopotamus.)

"He tells us there's never been a club running there. We hadn't been on that side of town for years, we knew there was a club but we couldn't think of the name. He says, 'Well, there's no clubs in this area so you're going in for loitering.' So we get inside the Seventeenth; we don't know any of the girls and the cops don't recognize us. We asked to speak to the sergeant. He was the type who would suck anything in and we almost had him convinced we weren't working girls. Then in comes this m.f. from Midtown North, *our* precinct.

"He says, 'Hi girls, weren't you all just in last night?'

"We knew we were through.

"The sergeant says, 'Looks like you blew it, huh?' "

As the prostitute sees it, the plainclothes are the only cops who make "righteous arrests" for the actual execution of her trade. Or in police parlance, the only cops who can make a true "pross collar" on a "direct" proposition to themselves or an "overheard" to a John. A fair contest. Uniformed officers can arrest only for "loitering for the purpose of prostitution," and if they are lazy or hungry for overtime, some will yank a vanful of familiar faces off the stools of Riker's in the middle of their coffee break.

"That's cheating," says a veteran pross. "They know we'll be out here rain, snow, sleet, hail—we work when the postman doesn't!"

The ugly combat is not between these two professional teams. It is played out on the street every night, after midnight, when the marginal hustlers come up from their concrete holes like worms in a warm rain to prey on the pross. Now the dedicated woman must compete with ripoff artists and fly-by-night whores who will mug or cut another girl as soon as a trick, and the "jive bitches" and "poop butts" who are on the street just for kicks, and the summer runaways from Connecticut who undercut fixed street prices, and the knobbers. Knobbers are female impersonators who do a brisk business as prostitutes in the hallways along Ninth and Tenth. *Damn knobbers strutting their silicone breasts past dumb Jersey truck drivers, the cops say they're better-looking than the real thing, it's an insult!* And the junkies: they lie in wait and watch how many tricks a girl takes into the hotel and when they figure she has enough for their fix, jump her. And pimply boys from Queens who still travel in groups, still giggle and brag; they always start trouble. On top of all this a girl must contend with the nightly complement of con men, assault and robbery men, cripples, crazies, drunks, punks, putrid old women with twelve shopping bags who pick at the streets like crows, and the welfare winos who persist in nursing their pints of Thunderbird in the doorways of working pross hotels.

Through this zoo walks the dedicated pross with a meter ticking under her skirt. And a carpet knife in her bag, for good reason. She is the fall guy, the flatbacker from whom a long line of men make their money, beginning with the hotel managers and ending with the Jewish Mafia owners safely sleeping out in Great Neck. She is the first to be picked up and the last to be paid. And during the mayor's annual cleanup campaign, she is the one most likely to end up dead.

Every summer brings out one killing trick. In 1970 he went exclusively for pregnant girls wearing wigs. After killing them he would cut them open and mutilate the fetus. But what really made it bad, says the girls, was he didn't even rob them. All he took was the wig for a memento. From his last victim he borrowed enough blood to write on the wall STOP ME BEFORE I DO IT AGAIN. In 1971 there was a trick around who specialized in surgery on the girls' throats, ear to ear. And in mid-July of 1972, the forty girls passing a restful night in the cells of Midtown North learned there was a new killer loose. The matron came back to ask if any of them had seen a well-known pross; she had been found dead at 5:00 A.M. in the back seat of a car parked in a West Side lot. Nobody knew a thing. Nobody ever does about murders among hustlers, although they represent a significant number of the homicides in Midtown North. It could have been the killing of a knobber, broken like a chicken bone by a mortified truck driver whose buddies told him he had been done by a "fag." An attempt was made to have it look as though the prostitute was killed by this year's freak trick, but the information developed by police from the street was that she was killed by a pimp.

Couldn't she have been murdered by an organization with major commercial interests in midtown sex? I asked, trying to sound knowledgeable. Sergeant Sidney Patrick, a droll young Welshman with guts and brains and family connections to our more colorful local Sicilian-Americans, sat me down for the first of a dozen spontaneous seminars.

"Obviously you are talking about the Mafia. You see, the massage parlors, the bookstores and the peep shows are all part of the Five Family interest in midtown. But they want nothing to do with street pross; they consider the pimps too stupid to deal with. Pimps kill their prostitutes. That's common. There have already been a number of beatings, bad beatings. Right now we're looking for King George. He's a pimp who punishes his girls by making them sit in a bathtub while he pours boiling water into it. We have a warrant against him on the complaint of a fifteen and a sixteen-year-old girl who have since been returned to Minneapolis."

"Minneapolis!" A familiar chord from my own research. "Many of the streetwalkers I've interviewed this summer come from Minneapolis."

"Everybody's from Minneapolis," the sergeant said dryly. "What you would expect to see now is a rash of killings whereby the pimps will demonstrate to the girls that they had better stop turning the pimps in."

Thus I learned one or two tricks built into this game of tag. When the mayor orders a crackdown on prostitution, the first thing that happens is robberies go *up*. A girl must meet her quota. No pimp will let her off the street and into bed until she has at least $200 to $250 in cash, and when push comes to shove, it is easier to rob than to flatback. As arrests rise, money tightens. Pimps step up their beatings. Girls rebel. Finally one of them violates the primal taboo and turns in her man. She has a wide selection of charges: assault, rape, sodomy, false imprisonment. Now it is the pimp's turn to sacrifice a girl to set an example. When the police begin finding pross laid out like Swiss cheese on the back seats of cars, everyone knows the game has turned mean. Such was the state of affairs in midsummer 1972.

Midtown North was due to be born on May 1. It was part of the "midtown concept," an idea conceived by New York's Chief of Patrol Donald Cawley which was to give special attention to the income-producing heart of the city. Times Square was about to throw a final fatal clot. Over the past five summers its major vessels—the entertainment, theater, hotel, and garment districts—had been clogging with prostitutes, criminals, and fear. Worst was the fear. It had affected tourists everywhere like an announcement of rat plague. Corporate officers were performing their own traumatic surgery, cutting out for the suburbs. If the heart of the city stopped beating, the tax base dried up, and that was the end of the game. Who goes to the Bronx?

The midtown concept held that the greater midtown area presented a unique policing problem: it was low on residents and high in crime. Two new macroprecincts were to be created and saturated with men. Six hundred cops were quietly "borrowed" from their posts in other boroughs and divided about equally between Midtown North and Midtown South. New maps were drawn; new cars, new vans, and new walkie-talkies purchased.

Midtown North was fleshed out with a new commander—Deputy Inspector Charles Peterson, whose master's thesis on "Specialization in Detective Function" was used recently to reorganize New York's Detective Bureau for the first time since 1919. Allocated to the area were 2 captains, 11 lieutenants, 54 sergeants, and 533 patrolmen. That meant a 130 percent increase of manpower, a total of 83 foot posts and 8 radio motor patrols to be concentrated on the reduction of violent crime, robbery, and loitering in the business and entertainment sectors. The Association for a Better New York contributed $3,000 for new collar insignias—brass pins with the words MIDTOWN NORTH. Charlie Peterson designed the insignia on a paper bag. All was ready for the twin birth on May 1. But Mayor Lindsay wasn't home to deliver Midtown North and South. He was out campaigning for the Presidency.

I phoned Inspector Peterson again a month later. Could we talk now about massage parlors?

"You'd better get down here before massage parlors become extinct," he bragged. "I've closed eighteen already, we only have six left."

The inspector was riding high that day in early June. His station house was crawling with cops. His arrest room was jammed with school desks, all filled with pouting prostitutes in Carmen Miranda wigs—it might have been after-school-time at Hollywood High. His sergeants were bristling with the latest reports from Peterson's own nine-man task force. In May, without waiting for any fancy public-relations name, they had come on like gangbusters: padlocking massage parlors, papering the windows of bookstores selling phony sex and bondage devices, carting pimp-mobiles off to the pound if they so much as double-parked to buy cigarettes, and giving the prostitutes no sleep at all.

Peterson's task force alone had scored 407 arrests for loitering for prostitution in May. On top of that, the pross van was scooping up at least 36 girls a night. Even the female impersonators were on the run. The inspector had created a "knob squad." Encouraging word was coming back from the street. With all the heat on massage parlors, their regular girls were quitting. Desperate managers were renting the vacant stalls to streetwalkers to do their Johns for $5 a go.

"I've only had five weeks of moving ahead and everybody's howling," the inspector smiled. "That makes me feel good."

Midtown North was operating purely on the force of Charlie Peterson's personality. MTN takes in roughly 60 subway platforms, nearly all prostitution, welfare and fat-cat convention hotels, most brassy restaurants, all Broadway theaters, 18 to 24 massage parlors, dozens of live peep shows and porno movies, and 700 bars—seven hundred! If the new Deputy Inspector had a drink in a different bar every working night, it would take him three years to cover his district. Instead, he takes the same quiet dinner table at the same steak house every night and dreams of dragging a giant magnet up Eighth Avenue. Phantasmagoria! "Thousands of guns would come out of the doorways and up through the subway grating with guys shouting, 'But I'm just minding this jacket for a friend, honest!' " Peterson laughs. He is no ordinary cop.

Charles Francis Peterson began work less than fifteen years ago in the West 30th Street precinct. A baby of twenty-four with detective rank. He held a law degree from St. John's, a master's degree in public administration from Michigan State, and a taste for opera. Raised by eleven tough old-time "Whaddya got, kid?" type detectives, he had to fight his way more than once out of the Wigwam Bar, slugging it out with Brooklyn's "high steel" Indian bridge workers. As a reward the detectives always gave him opera openings. "Send the kid, he likes that fag stuff." No one knew exactly what to make of the boy wonder. They still don't. He turns out to be a gingery Irish Catholic egghead with a memory like an elephant, a mind as orderly as Kissinger's, the devil's wit, a saint's compassion, and an unreasonable devotion to his $25,000-a-year job.

About his mission in Midtown North he was dead clear that first day. "I'm here to clean up midtown so the tourists will keep coming back, the New Yorkers will stay, and the corporate offices won't leave." Did he have a solution to the prostitution problem? He didn't bat an eye. "Every commuter should take one home."

A week later Deputy Inspector Peterson showed signs of the inevitable wear and tear from pross-chasing. "You can't wipe them out. It's like the old game of Ringaleveo. Every night this station house is filled. Next day they come back from court, freshen up and at three-thirty they rush out to their posts as if a gun was fired—it's a new game, same players!"

Prostitution represents only 5 percent of the problems in MTN. But more than half of its robberies are pross-related. Peterson's problem with the pross was not moral, it was criminal. The moth-and-flame theory: both prostitutes and pornography attract to the area undesirables who prey on other undesirables. MTN had become the pimp headquarters of the Western world, for example. Staring the station house right in the face, on the corner of Eighth Avenue and 54th Street, is the Westerly Apartment House, a high-rise home/office to something like a hundred pimps. The oldest and most venerated of them all, Eddie Frierson, occupies the "executive suite" on the eighteenth floor. Woody's, Tommy Small, and Angel's West—all hustling pimp bars—operate within a few blocks of the inspector's office. Since 99 percent of Manhattan's pimps are black, the favorite recreation to pass all those monotonous hours in the bars is to mock, bait, and tease white cops. It can get on an inspector's nerves.

The cast of The Harem, a massage parlor, is in the inspector's arrest room again. He phones the judge: why can't these girls be sentenced to eight hours in the precinct's cells? The judge says Peterson has no facilities for serving them meals.

"What is this, a federal pen? I'll *buy* them dinner. I'll give them six hours in the basement with a deck of cards. Otherwise their Johns are going to get robbed!"

The judge is not impressed. And so the girls will go downtown and through the revolving-door justice of our Criminal Court system and before the arresting officers leave the courthouse, the girls will be back in business.

Peterson met with Mayor Lindsay in mid-June. He was given a green light to expand his experimental task force into a capital-letter multiagency Code Enforcement Team composed of inspectors from Health, Fire, Building, Sanitation, and Consumer Affairs. But even then Peterson's reservations had the solid quality of prophecy. "If you're going to have a real midtown cleanup, why not give ten policemen, firemen and building inspectors status as special assistants to the mayor—doing the *mayor's* work—and get the state attorney general in on it, get the tax people in on it, and then have all the cases go before the same panel of judges? Times Square could be a park in six months."

Peterson could speak with authority on the frustration of dealing with city judges, being himself a lawyer. "Their judicial qualifications don't mean a damn. A judge is a lawyer who once knew a governor. After they reach their 'sandwich quota,' they can dismiss and suspend and adjourn all the cases we bring in. It's pitiful how much manpower I spend down in that court."

Discipline around Midtown North was just as vigorous as around Della Bella's hotels. At precisely four each day, the new shift of Midtown North men would assemble in a block of blue before the deputy inspector, who would formally "turn out" his troops. The ritual took thirty minutes, a curious limbo during which, I noticed, day-shift girls did a particularly brisk business. One day a patrolman leaned out of formation to explain, "The hookers turn out half an hour before we do."

I was introduced to Sergeant Hanson, supervisor of the original precinct task force. He looked tired. He had been playing this futile game for eight months. His experience with midtown prostitutes confirmed my own observations: over 60 percent are white. Most seem to come from Minneapolis with a baby on their knee, or at least pregnant. The young white girls are rarely on drugs. Some are very intelligent. All are better-looking than average.

"I've met some from doctors' families," Sergeant Hanson said. "I'm sure they could do very well on the outside."

"Why would they do this if they could do something else for nearly the same money?" I asked.

"That's a question I've been trying to answer for eight months." The sergeant was a compassionate man, but limited to a jailhouse view of prostitutes. He gave the best guess he could: "Possibly it's the easy way out."

Chapter Four

She was a white girl saddled with an
illegitimate child. In Hell's Bedroom,
most girls are.
She had a goal—a business or a home
of her own someday. Most girls do.
She has been through five years and
six pimps and has gone exactly nowhere.
Most girls don't.
By the time I met her, it was too late to
change what Hell's Bedroom had done to
a nice girl like ...

MINNESOTA MARSHA

Minnesota, Michigan, Massachusetts, Ohio—these are
the four states, in order, with the largest direct pipe-
lines sending white prostitutes to New York. Although
it has not yet reached academia, a startling conclusion
emerges, based on street-level experience recounted by
patrolmen who have operated the prostitution van over
the past four years, and by Sergeants Patrick and
Hanson of Midtown North, as well as six months of
my own interviews and observations on Manhattan's
West Side. That conclusion reflects the racial confu-
sion and ethnic backlash of our times.

The girls are raised in predominantly black neigh-
borhoods or mixed—but not integrated—poor white
and black sections of the major cities of these states.
Or in the black pocket suburbs just outside them.

Their earliest sexual experiences are with their school-mates, often black boys, which for them is a natural occurrence. Hungry for love, the girls seldom take precautions. Before they become adults they become pregnant.

The parents involved rarely share the young couple's healthy color-blindness. They cannot separate the physical predicament from the racial fears and furies it provokes. To a girl's struggling white ethnic parents, and often to the boy's striving black parents, there is nothing romantic or salvageable about it; all they see is an illegitimate child with half-brown skin. The girl is expelled from school or taken out by her parents and sent to work. Overnight she becomes a social pariah in her own neighborhood. With her education stunted, what can she do? Dragging a baby from room to rented room, she finds it impossible to work and scarcely worth living.

Girls often "turn out" first at home, only to find that prostitution laws are stiffer and more rigidly enforced in places like Minneapolis. A girl found guilty of "gross common prostitution" there may be given a year and a day in the workhouse *and* a $1,000 fine. What happens next is not due to any predisposition of cities like Detroit, Boston and Minneapolis to produce prostitution-prone children; it's accidental. It merely means there has been a historical link set up, and it works like this:

One day a former girl friend who went through the same mill comes back from New York. She is transformed. Flashy clothes, platform shoes, her teeth capped, and no baby pulling on her sleeve! She describes glowingly the very special kind of *family* life provided by a pimp. Of course it is the pimp who sent her back home to recruit. He puts up his stable of two or three girls in a respectable high-rise apartment, pays their rent, buys them clothes and divides his affections by sleeping with a different one each night. The tie that really binds is what the pimp promises to do for the prostitute's child: he *understands;* most of his girls have half-black children. (Almost to a man, New York pimps are black.) Number one, he will be a father-substitute. Number two, he provides a babysitter, and this is what frees his girls to work. The package, though loaded, is irresistible.

This was all reliable street-level research, but it didn't really make sense until I met Marsha. It was June 22, 1972. I had been riding the pross van all night with "Muscles," "Wimpy" and "Lurch"—known colloquially as the "pussy posse"—and listening to Patrolman Bill Chepil, who had commanded this wayward bus for the past four years.

"They have so many aliases, it's outrageous," he was saying. "We have to take whatever name they give the arresting officer—they have an I.D. for every day of the week."

How often does he arrest the John?

"Never. It's impossible. We wear uniforms. We telegraph ourselves a mile away."

I referred to the 1967 change in the penal code which makes patronizing a prostitute a violation.

"What's patronizing?" Patrolman Chepil gave a first-rate imitation of the D.A.'s office throwing charges back in his face. "Is it a verbal agreement? Is it after the money is passed? Is it after the act is committed?"

"There goes a knobber," someone interrupts. Chepil pounces on the gas pedal and the van leapfrogs after the suspect with all the subtlety of a Donald Duck cartoon chase. Suspect and John part company. Van jumps the curb. Suspect totters toward the van in ankle-strap heels, displaying the most beautiful legs since Dietrich was insured, and thrusts out a home-made card:

CERTIFYED COMPANY ID CARD
TOI WALKER
CLERCK TYPIST

"I'm a fella," she/he purrs engagingly. "My real name's Jerry, like in Jerome."

"What were you talking to that trick about?"

"The weather."

"Then why are you out here every night?"

"I'm a star in the Jewel Box Revue."

"Are those your titties?"

"Sure. Hormone shots. Told you I was a fella."

Nothing about the game works the way the words of the penal code spell it out. Patrolman Chepil hoists back into the van.

"They're all crazy, all have a tale," he says with good-natured resignation. "Ninety-nine percent of them you can't trust. Especially the new ones—real terrorists. But there's always one or two. I'll try to find Marsha for you. She's straight."

The long thin girl was wearing long thin earrings—ivory elephants dangling on gold chains—for good luck. We found her near dawn in the deserted canyon of Eighth Avenue. She was swaying gracefully by the curbstone like some exotic nightbloom that grows wild in cement and survives on city poisons. She has left five years of her life on these pavingstones. To show for it she has twenty-seven direct prostitution arrests, one grand larceny conviction and a vague memory of being picked up by the pross van roughly fifteen hundred times. Marsha is her day name. Sandy is her night name. Her real name is impenetrably Polish and she is white and of course she comes from Minneapolis. This night, for safety only, her companion is the plump, moist Valerie.

It is a silly question to ask a prostitute why she does it. The top salary for a teacher with a BA in New York City public schools is $13,950; for a registered staff nurse, $13,000; for a telephone operator, about $8,000. The absolute daily minimum a pimp expects a streetwalker to bring in is $200 a night. That comes to easily $70,000 a year. These are the highest-paid "professional" women in America.

Marsha answers the question without my asking: "Everyone in life has a goal they want to reach. Prostitutes too. This is the fastest way of getting money as a woman, by using your best years to sell what you can sell the easiest. You look at people that work jobs every day, like a waitress or a bellhop—they have to work nineteen or twenty *years* for what we can make in a year, maybe even in six months."

Six months?

Marsha tucks her lower lip behind her teeth, almost modestly. "I work twelve hours a day. When I was on top, before this crackdown on prostitution, if I lucked up I could make ten grand in a month."

But rare is the streetwalker who keeps any of her money. This leaves everyone, including policemen who have spent years riding the pross van, confounded. And so I ask again, as I have asked so many girls: How much of this money do you turn over to your pimp, and why?

"I give him *all* of it," Valerie breaks in with her half-lunatic eyes blazing. She is the former addict with only nine months in this game, and she wants to talk:

"I never had a man before. I worked independent. But I love it, I love it! Because he gives me en-ee-thing I want, a new outfit, silver jewelry. I've only got one wife-in-law, and I'm the first one of his girls she's ever gotten along with. We both have separate apartments on the East Side. He spends tonight with me, tomorrow with her and so on. That's why I know whatever we have together is mine, all *mine*."

To Valerie (as to most street girls), the pimp is still sacred, a superbeing created in her own desperate brain in whom she is investing all hopes, dreams and goals for the future. She wears his beatings proudly as symbols of affection. He is the father-substitute; he disciplines, he cares. She submits gladly to his sadistic lovemaking. The pimp as lover takes her money, tricks her, gives her raw sex but denies her an ounce of emotion, and drops her ten minutes later for another woman—exactly reversing the sadomasochistic process she must play with her own tricks. In this way she can reaffirm herself (at least every other night) as that adoring, devoted, sacrificial lamb—the "feminine" woman. Prostitutes are unbelievably romantic. There is one sentence they all utter with total conviction: "I couldn't stand to live and sleep with someone I didn't love—*I gotta love him!*"

"There goes my man in the green Eldorado." Valerie wriggles all over and points like a dog on the hunt. "See him parking at the end of the block? Probably cutting reefer."

What does her man do, I ask.

"He doesn't do *nothing*. But the way he does nothing is *beautiful*."

Valerie is still new enough to labor under the standard fantasy of a prostitute's future with her pimp. "I want my daughter back. So my man and I will drive down and kidnap her from that welfare family . . . and then my man will have to get me a bigger apartment —it might cost $600—and then I'll drop her with a baby-sitter while I work days and my man will watch her at night. He'll save my money. Someday we'll get a business—"

"—A restaurant or a little boutique, right?" Marsha completes the fantasy for her friend. Valerie nods vigorously. "And if not a business, someday he'll get you a home, right?" Again the girl nods. The goals are always, pathetically, the same.

"I don't care how many girls you ask," Marsha turned to me to add, "wherever you ask them, Los Angeles or Eighth Avenue, not one girl has an explanation for her pimp. My goal was to take two or three grand and put it down in a business. But the main thing is, being a prostitute and having a record, you have a hard time getting credit."

In her five years on the street Marsha has run through six pimps and watched hundreds of babies like Valerie turn old, bitter, and broke.

"Ain't nobody out there your friend," she says, letting down her words with the dull thud of unburdened experience. "The only really good friend you got, to tell you the truth, is your man. If he isn't your friend—"

Marsha turned, directing my eyes to the obvious. We looked down the long ugly blacktop desert that is Eighth Avenue at four in the morning.

"—you ain't got nobody."

The veteran doesn't cry anymore, she doesn't even kick much. But there are small, telling signs that most of the spirit and all of the illusions have gone out of her work. She no longer bothers to curl her hair. She has lost track of her little black cashbook, along with her ex-pimp; Marsha never tries to recover such things. Her losses are too painful to face.

And some nights when she is all played out, when not even her own man wants her, when the wheel of street fortune turns and jams and turns up new faces and keeps turning, she tries to escape into a restaurant and have a quiet supper. An innocent John stops by to ask the price. She breaks a chair over his head.

"If a girl were to come up to me today and say 'I want to be a prostitute,' I'd tell her, 'No matter how bad it is, go back home.'"

Sgt. Hanson's observation, that prostitutes might just be looking for the easy way out, could apply to Valerie. Her father is a foreign trade expert in the Nixon Administration; he has had two wives in addition to this daughter who ran delinquent at the age of thirteen. But at least she had a father *there*.

Marsha's home life could have been worse, but not much. Over the days, as we talked, she parted with her memories in bursts and silences—the small hidden agonies would explode, followed by lakes in the conversation meant to cover despair. These colorless lakes were blanketed by expressions such as "this 'n' that" or "See, so." That was the only way Marsha could tell me how it was back home, by pretending to herself it wasn't that bad.

"We started with six kids in the family. We lived twenty or thirty miles outside Minneapolis, they call that Coon Rapids. I was the youngest. Then my two closest sisters took me out drinkin' in Anoka County with a bunch of guys one night and they got killed. See, so.

". . . the rest of us kids stuck together after that. We

didn't have much to do with our parents because my ma was an alcoholic and she had cancer of the breast and she had an operation on that. And then she had ulcers and they took a third of her stomach out. Then she had cancer of the female organs, they had to come out too. All this happened from the time I was ten to thirteen.

"Then ma got in the habit of using these drugs, see so.

". . . they must have been heavy barbiturates, the hospital gave them to her when she came home to dope her up. Got so she'd just have to have them. Us kids would throw them down the toilet. My dad got so he couldn't be around her. So he started goin' out with other women, this 'n' that.

". . . in the last three years, I'd say, my father has been making a rerun of my mother's life. He started the pills, the alcohol, and now he's in the same position—he's useless. Last time I was back home [she left New York in February of 1972 and tried to stick it out in Minneapolis for three months] they had him in the state hospital. He escaped from there and got lost and they found him in the International Airport Hotel. He'd eaten a lot of pills and drunk a lot of liquor so I guess he got in one of his depressed moods. 'Cause they found him trying to cut his wrists.

"We were glad when ma and daddy split up. Us girls and our mom moved to the city. Ma was getting welfare. How much I don't know. She'd take the welfare checks and cash them, and we wouldn't see her for two, three weeks. She'd be out on a drunk, this 'n' that.

". . . one morning I heard the fire engines. She'd fallen asleep on the couch with a cigarette. So there went everything we had. See, so."

And then Marsha would play quietly for a while

with her white elephant earrings, like the little girl she never had the chance to be.

One evening we were touring around Hell's Bedroom together in the back of a cab. We'd decided Marsha should give me a hooker's guide to Times Square. She was alive, laughing, issuing commands to the cab driver the way only a prostitute can do; she was in control. All at once her mind leaped back to another car, another rejection. . . . She was in high school and her aunt had taken in the family after the fire. But Marsha's was always the "down-rated family" of all the Polish relatives. Her aunt kept calling Marsha and her sisters "a bunch of sluts" because they had some friends and laughs; her children didn't. One night the aunt threw them all out of the house. They went to their mother's room to appeal for help; where could they stay now? The mother was in bed at the time. Their only remaining possession was a raunchy old car parked in a lot behind the aunt's house. The mother coaxed her four daughters to go outside and sit in the car. She would be out in a few minutes.

"We waited and waited and waited," Marsha says, recalling that first night in the car, as if still groping for some rationale, some handle to the chaos that went by the name home life. "Ma never came out. So I went in to see for myself. She had gone back to sleep.

"Next day, to make it look good, she brought us some rolls and lunchmeat. We made our own sandwiches in the car. Ma said she was going to the Cities to find us all a place to stay. She kept telling us she couldn't find a good enough place, this 'n' that.

"Me and my sisters—Gerry, June and Marge—we all slept in the car behind my aunt's house for four months."

And then our cab passed the Raymona Hotel and

Marsha had to get out and go back to work.

Other nights, when the sirens outside were incessant or when she was too tired and sore to spend another night in a jail cell, she would come to my apartment to talk. From here on, hers was a classic progression story:

"When I was sixteen, my first boy friend and I skipped school for a week while his parents were out of town. He was a track star and his folks were very, very religious. Evangelists in fact. When his dad came back, he told the school I was a bad influence on the boy. They expelled me. *Me,* and the boy was colored, but like I said it was a Negro school [Central High in South Minneapolis]. In the meantime, I didn't know it but I was pregnant. I was outside playing basketball, football—name it and I was doing it—rolling down hills and all. I hadn't had my period for two months but I didn't really pay attention to it. Maybe my system was just changing. It was—well, he was my first boy friend. I figured it was all right. We had gone together for a year.

"About two months after I had the baby, he decided to call it quits. I guess he was finding a different life or something. I don't know. I didn't really bother to ask him. I kept thinking he would come around to marry me, but then, see, he was the type of person, the same night I had his baby in the hospital, he was out having sex with somebody else. By the time you find out, what can you do? Holler at him? Hit on him? It won't do you any good because it's over and done with.

"My baby stays with his parents. He's got himself a little Afro, not too dark and not too light. His father's married now, and his wife just had a baby. I went over to pay my respects when I was home in February. I was the last person he expected to see. But I might as well act like a human being. Being bitter won't get me anywhere, won't get him anywhere, won't get the baby anywhere."

On the inside of her knee, Marsha's first pimp left his brand: three tatooed initials. They met on the streets of Minneapolis. Two people going nowhere; he already had a record. The difference between them, which brought them together, is not dissimilar from the bond between many couples. He assumed the role of Marsha's older brother, protecting her from the attacks of a hostile outside world, and simultaneously disposing of his own feelings of self-abasement by subjecting her to his aggression.

"My first pimp got to know my baby and accepted him as his own son. To this day he calls him his own son. But that's rare. A lot of pimps will say 'I'll do this 'n' that for your baby,' but after they get the woman, and the woman starts making money, they neglect the baby. Some will let you send so much money home a month. I used to send $100 or $150, but it wasn't any kind of money you could keep. The pimp goes right to Western Union with you to make sure it's going to the kid.

"Home is where your pimp is. You see, everybody thinks a pimp beats a girl day and night, takes her money and that's it. But if you stick with a pimp long enough, you can touch his heart. My ex-pimp made arrangements where he could have two wife-in-laws for *us*, and keep me to the side for himself. It worked on and off as long as the other girls didn't catch on that they were being used. Just to make it look good, I worked the street too.

"You could say I'm in love with my ex-pimp. You could say he was in love with me."

They split up because of the inevitable rumors, suspicions, accusations. He was sure she had turned lesbian. She imagined his fickle eye was drifting toward a wife-in-law. As Marsha expresses it, the loss of one's first pimp—that last vestige of innocence and dreams of future security—leaves a premature scar on the emotions from which there is no escape, only a calculated repetition.

"All men are alike. They think a prostitute can't be faithful. They see another pimp messing around with their woman and right away they think she's bargaining to give him some of the action. And then a lot of girls will just go and lie about their wife-in-laws to stir up trouble and try and take over the top woman's place. This type of life changes your attitude completely. It turns you into a cold, hard person. You'll do anything just to get money."

Money buys the pimp's "love." In all the conversations with prostitutes it always comes down to that. The enemy is time. At first a pimp is grateful for the money his woman brings in. As he builds a stable, his affections are drawn toward the best earners, who are inevitably younger. Intimidated, his top woman must either match them or recruit even fresher talent to supplement her own earnings. I asked Marsha if she didn't ever feel just plain jealous.

"At first it's hard to accept the fact of your man being with another woman. Eventually you see they are helping you. The more money the other girls bring in, the less pressure falls on you. You not only want wife-in-laws, you begin bringing the best-looking girls on the street home to your man."

In straight life, this corresponds to the woman who says to her daughter, "I wish I had a nice fresh young girl to send into your father." In the competitive circus that is street life, this painful tightrope can be

HUSTLING

walked only so long. Rarely does a prostitute end up
with her original pimp. When he drops her, she cus-
tomarily sends her next pimp to smash the apartment
of her rival. Or commits suicide. Marsha simply en-
dured.

"I used to keep track day to day of what I made.
Kept it all in a little black book for my own benefit. I
had to know if I was gaining, prospering, or if I was
losing the touch. One night your ambition can be way
up and in a second flat it can be knocked down. If I
was in a good mood, I'd talk a trick into staying a while
and spending an extra hundred. Other days, when
you're feeling like a low-down dirty bitch, you cut your
time short. Some tricks will call you a slut or stinkin'
whore. It might bother you at the moment, but you
just turn around and say [Marsha struck a pose of hit-
and-run contempt]: 'You're the sucker, not me, I've
got your money. You ain't got nothing!'

"I used to keep track of it all, but when my ex and
I split up I left my little book behind. I've had four or
five men since then. There's no plan. I live more or
less day by day."

Marsha's voice loses speed, as though two or three
of her batteries had gone dead. We had talked another
night away and the city dawn fell harsh across her
face. She spun out her last, shaky philosophy.

"This type of life is more or less depressing. I mean
it has its good points and it has its bad points. You can
be happy and you can be sad. It's the type of life
where your mind is never really at ease."

I walked Marsha back to the Raymona Hotel. She
slipped behind the windowed door like a picture into
a frame. Shattered, aimless, older, wiser, trapped, or
what they call on the street that is consuming her—a
"dedicated woman."

Chapter Five

A long line of men make their money from
the streetwalker, beginning with her pimp
and ending with the property owners safely
sleeping out in suburbia. They will lie to
keep themselves out of print. They will
plead no profit, no responsibility, no power
under existing law, when in fact they have
all three. The nature of the beast is, in a
word, greed. Somebody out there does not
want our central cities cleaned up. In New
York we call them . . .

THE LANDLORDS
OF HELL'S BEDROOM

No one in city government was willing to talk about
the landlords of Hell's Bedroom. Prostitutes, pimps,
the popcorn sellers in porno movie houses, yes—arrest the vermin—but don't mention the names of *owners*. It was a bizarre discrimination between the sacred
and the profane, yet one so firmly rooted in political
tradition, the public scarcely noticed.

Mayor Lindsay's Times Square Development Council had been meeting since February 1972. That meant
that selected citizens with major self-interests in midtown, such as restaurateur Vincent Sardi and landlords Seymour Durst, Jerome Minskoff, and Bob Tisch,
a smattering of union and theater people, and a few
"quasi members" from the Police, Sanitation, Corporation Counsel, and Consumer Affairs departments,

had gathered together in Executive Director William Bardel's office, hit-and-miss, and had quasi-attacked the problem of cleaning up midtown. They invented names for police action like "Operation T." They issued bogeyman phrases like "intensive enforcement." And now it was June.

—All twenty-four massage parlors were back in action in Midtown North, the newborn macro-precinct beefed up with 140 percent more men. Deputy Inspector Charles Peterson had closed all but six of them in May with his own no-name task force, but without help in enforcement from other city agencies it was a daily game of tag. And to the fiery Peterson's chagrin, he was losing.

—The peep shows were all but impregnable. The last time Inspector Peterson saw a "stag" movie the girls wore pearls and the men wore black socks and there weren't more than twenty films making the rounds of greater Brooklyn. Now they were full-color thrillers projected inside a coin-operated box and featuring lusty young hippies and heads who perform for kicks, not money (film makers who advertise for talent in *Screw* say they have to beat the kids off with sticks). Today the Organized Crime Control Bureau estimates there are more than one thousand of these machines in New York City. Every two minutes, at one erotic threshold or another, the screen goes dark. It demands another quarter, another, another—until the customer is so engrossed his pocket could be picked by an elephant. But while the city awaited rulings from the Supreme Court on new obscenity standards, the padlocking of peep shows and seizure of films was another silly game of tag. Police seized. Peep shows sued.

Live sex shows and pornographic movie houses

were putting away staggering profits. It appeared that America's favorite passive sport—Sunday afternoons titillating over TV "highlights" of pro football half-backs being maimed—was about to be replaced by spectator sex.

—Hotel operator Jimmy Della Bella's fleabags, the Raymona and the Lark, were flourishing, as were other prostitution hotels in and around Eighth Avenue. Since no one else would talk, I tried out my questions on the prosperous hotelkeeper, Jimmy Della Bella.

Prostitution could not exist without the property and protection of wealthy businessmen and organized crime, I reminded him. What about the big fish who own the real estate in which their leaseholders operate the prostitution hotels and strings of massage parlors and peep shows?

"Just like a guy who has a string of supermarkets, it's a business," was the Della Bella rationale. "If he runs it in a right way, eh, what's the difference? Number one, do you feel anyone's hurtin'?"

The prostitutes and the taxpayers, I suggest, and the courts and the police. Isn't it lunacy to have the police and prostitutes playing this expensive game of tag around town and tying up the courts, while organized criminals and prominent businessmen are left alone to make millions on midtown prostitution and pornography?

"Why shouldn't the prostitutes go to jail?" Della Bella asked.

"If the mayor decided to crack down on gambling at the race track, *would he put the race horses in jail?*" I answered.

Della Bella said he could see my logic. "But hey, the Hotel Association is making money from it. The cops are gettin' rich too, whaddaya think? Overtime.

Believe me, to keep the pross off the streets, it's cost-
ing this precinct here from eighteen to twenty thousand dollars a *week*."

Meanwhile *Variety* headlines weekly predicted
doom for Times Square. The theater people were
screaming. Real-estate barons such as Jerry Minskoff,
who had sunk $140 million into the winged office
tower at One Astor Plaza and who took a heroic gamble on giving Broadway its first new legitimate theater
in thirty-five years, began to perspire heavily. His office tower stood one-third empty.

Thus far the only important development had been
an injunction brought by six massage parlors *against*
—believe it or not—John Lindsay, both as mayor and
individually; Patrick Murphy, both as police commissioner and individually; Fire Commissioner Robert
Lowery and Buildings Department Commissioner Joseph Stein. The charge was harassment. The affidavits
were signed by a janitor and the Misses Nephertita
Kramer and Ronnel Von Klaussen—both convicted
prostitutes.

But the federal judge had been at pains to protect
the civil liberties of those who swore out the affidavits.
That left Inspector Peterson to a battle of nerves with
the likes of lawyers Kassner and Detsky.

The Robert Halls of the legal profession, as they
proudly refer to themselves, Herbert Kassner and Seymour Detsky specialize in defense of massage parlors, peep shows, live sex shows, pornographic movie
houses, and the plain pipe-rack pornographer. The
mayor's 1972 cleanup probably made their careers.
The injunction against Lindsay et al. was their hand-
iwork. They made Peterson a "good faith" offer,
Kassner and Detsky style. They would ask their mas-

sage parlors to keep a guest book.

Fuming, Inspector Peterson threw a copy of the injunction across his desk.

"I say this robbery cartel has got to go!" he said to me. "We've had cops walk into these massage parlors and catch the girls right in the act of sodomy. It's wide open."

An informant had reported the fees: "$10 to beat the meat, $20 for a blow job and $30 for a screw."

But morality was not the inspector's concern. Massage parlors generate many robbery and larceny complaints.

A new massage parlor was under construction on Eighth Avenue. Sergeant Sidney Patrick phoned the real estate agent listed on the door to inquire who would be legally occupying the building. The name was familiar: lawyer Seymour Detsky, under the corporation name of Ashland Hills Estates, Inc. His interest in the sex industry apparently was not limited to legal representation. Another of Kassner and Detsky's extracurricular activities is to send articles to publications, such as the one received by *New York* magazine condemning the *New York Times* for judging the people who patronize these establishments "and derive education, psychological, or entertaining value therefrom." It also flatly stated that "a myth being foisted on the public is that the streets of mid-Manhattan are unsafe for pedestrian traffic," and finally pontificated about the need to divest our city of its "Gestapo" of self-appointed guardians of the public morality.

Beyond writing their own public relations copy, the lawyers of Hell's Bedroom were given another reason to burn the midnight oil in their Empire State Building offices. Every night at six without fail, Kassner &

Detsky would get a phone call from Midtown North. (Inspector Peterson on the line with some obscure new challenge.) "Have you checked the Cosmetology Act?"

Kassner would call Detsky to the phone. Detsky never heard of the Cosmetology Act either. Out came the Tums. Out came the law books. Detsky would tell Kassner to cancel the Mah-Jongg game. "That crazy Peterson is on the phone again."

The Mafia has had a long romance with the prostitution business. The brothels of Chicago's Levee owed their world-famous opulence to maintenance by bosses Big Jim Colosimo and Al Capone, who took 25 percent off the top of their profits. In New York, underworld control of prostitution was solid until 1936. Lucky Luciano, keeper of a dazzling string of call girls, clashed that year with young turk Thomas E. Dewey. The special prosecutor not only nailed him on charges of compulsory prostitution, he shook the criminal world by sending Luciano away for thirty to fifty years.

After floundering on the outskirts of the sex industry for thirty years, the underworld presumably rejoiced in May 1967, when a series of Supreme Court decisions eased restrictions on obscenity. One decision reversed a conviction against a peep show. Wasting no more than a few months, organized crime moved full speed into the midtown pornography business. Mayor Lindsay's reaction at that time was: "We can live with the Supreme Court decision on pornography and obscenity." When a state commission investigating racketeer infiltration into the city's sex industry urged in 1970 that peep shows be required to be licensed as places of amusement—exactly the legislation the Mayor later proposed—Lindsay flatly refused.

By 1972, police estimated that three of New York's five major crime families were responsible for 90 percent of the pornography in the metropolitan area: the three family heads are Carmine Tramunti, Samuel (Sam the Plumber) De Cavalcante and Joseph Colombo.

A comeback in the prostitution business took longer. Only in the last two years has organized crime regained a strong foothold here—courtesy of the massage parlors. A seedy lot they are compared with the old Levee bordellos, but the concept is roughly the same. The massage parlor is a hit-and-run brothel, combining the virtues of low overhead and high turnover.

"There are two situations which are apparent in the massage parlor operations," Sergeant Patrick observed after inspecting every parlor in Midtown North three times a week for a couple of months. "One, they are all managed by the same overlord. Other than the four 'high-class' ones—Fifth Season, The Magic Carpet, Relaxation Plus and Caesar's Retreat—they are pretty well tied in to one organization. We're not on top of that information yet, but we're getting closer." The other apparent gimmick is the use of attorneys as a front. The incorporation papers carry not the names of the actual owners, but the names of their lawyers.

The Harem is the clearest case in point. It is a combination massage parlor, peep show, and bookstore at 723 Eighth Avenue. The attorneys for the landlord were Kassner and Detsky. Inspector Peterson learned from an informant that the operators of The Harem were George Kaplan and Joseph Gomberg, both known to law enforcement officers as being connected to the Mafia.

"K.O. Kaplan," a former California prize fighter, stands six feet four inches with a pair of hands the size of bowling balls. The history of violence in those hands begins with an arrest in 1954 for assault and from there it goes its colorful way to 1968, when Kaplan was charged with felony murder. He was alleged to have beaten a man to death with his bare hands. A grand jury did not return an indictment, and the district attorney had to drop the charge. Last summer, according to Sergeant Patrick, the massage parlor people threw a big party for K.O. Kaplan. He had just come back from Boston, bragging about beating another charge for committing homicide with his big bare bowling-ball hands.

Kaplan and Gomberg's overboss in The Harem was peep-show king Martin Hodas. In 1970 a State Commission of Investigation prepared an extensive report showing that much of the profit of the midtown sex industry was, even then, flowing directly or indirectly to organized crime. Three Hodas corporations, which represented almost the entire peep-show industry in New York at the time, were also detailed. (I later brought this intriguing report along to a meeting with the city's corporation counsel and his top staff. None of them had ever heard of it.)

On most of his obscenity arrests and indictments as a porno entrepreneur, with the help of lawyers Kassner and Detsky, Mr. Hodas was accustomed to walking out on bail, slapping a suit on city officials for harassment, and heading home to his estate forty miles away, in Lawrence, Long Island. The estate was succinctly described by a police officer who later arrested Hodas for attempted bribery. When he pushed the bell, it took longer for the chimes to stop ringing than it took to drive there from midtown.

The scene of a garish murder of a pimp and prostitute one recent Christmas Eve was the nouveau-posh East Side highrise at 157 East 57th Street. It was inside apartment 11-F, occupied by "Mr. Smith" and his pross, that Patrolman William Phillips allegedly committed the double killing. Since the hung jury was dismissed, no retrial has been set.

Mid-July. Open conflict breaks out on 49th Street. A busload of matrons from the suburbs is parked in front of the Eugene O'Neill Theater. The matinee is over and they are bored and hot. Across the street, in front of the Raymona Hotel, stands a lithe young prostitute. The bus driver swaggers over like Gregory Peck in *Duel in the Sun.*

"How much?"

"Twenty and ten."

"Twenty and ten!" (The $10 is always for the room.)

"If you don't want to buy it, just stay out of my face."

"One of those hard broads, huh!"

"Right, and I can get crazy too."

It is Marsha from Minneapolis, the veteran street girl I first met in May. Marsha of the white elephant earrings and quick Polish temper. Since then it had scarcely been possible to cross 49th Street without seeing her face, framed in the familiar windowed door of Della Bella's flagship pross hotel.

The driver climbs back into the bus and the matrons are all agog. "How much?" "What does she charge?" They flutter to the windows gawking, giggling, pointing, transported by the raw street tawdriness of it all. One stout old dreadnought calls out: "Is that all you charge, *thirty* dollars?"

The most sensitive issue for a prostitute is respect.

With straight people, deviants are at pains to legitimize themselves. Now here was a busload of married women, natural poison to a prostitute, who had jarred a hooker's precarious sense of self-respect. When Marsha rocketed up the steps of their bus, I knew she was about to shove every word down their throats.

"Listen, you got a lot of nerve to sit on this bus and mock me, when I got enough nerve to stand out here day and night to sell my body for money. Remember this about the thirty dollars I get, bitch. It comes out of your husband's paycheck once a week! And if it ain't in my pocket, it's in the next girl's pocket!"

Aghast, the matrons fall back on platitudes about the evils of selling one's flesh.

"Honey, I'd rather sell it than lay up in bed every day and worry about my bills being paid because my husband's taking thirty dollars out to pay a pross. I know where my money's coming from. You don't!"

Whipped and beaten, the matrons drop weakly into their seats. But Marsha was like a dog with a slipper. *This midtown cleanup has gone far enough.* Now she is up and down the aisle lecturing about the prostitute's social contribution, the plight of the American husband, the lack of class evidenced by the matron's clothes. And one final blow:

"If you had any sense, you bitches, you'd have done what I'm doing in your younger age. Right now your husbands might not be working some dumb job. They'd be laying up on your money, retired!"

The bus driver, unable to contain himself, applauded.

July 27. The mayor calls a press conference to announce a coordinated attack on the problems of pornography, massage parlors, prostitution hotels, and drug traffic in midtown. Promises are made. . . . Still, no one in city government was willing to talk about the *owners* of prostitution hotels. It was all very embarrassing. A little research turned up the names of immaculate East Side WASPS, bona fide members of the Association for a Better New York and the Mayor's own Times Square Development Council, a prominent Great Neck heart surgeon . . . several Park Avenue banks . . . the names Kassner and Detsky again.

The Raymona and the Lark hotels were still going strong. These were the two hustlingest pross hotels on Eighth Avenue which I had observed all summer.

Owner of the Raymona Hotel property is Ian Woodner, a Madison Avenue builder of high social polish and even higher self-regard. He owns it as president of the 50-50 Corporation, which leases the hotel to Raymona Associates, Inc. But then Raymona Associates turns out to be a front for one Joseph Rutkowski, who actually holds the lease on both the Raymona and the Lark—with Della Bella as his silent partner in the Lark. No one could have known this without digging for several months—but that is, of course, the point. The mortgage on the Raymona is held by Security National Bank on Park Avenue. On July 28 I phoned Ian Woodner at the 660 Madison Avenue offices of Jonathan Woodner Company, a family company. Here is the way part of the interview went:

Q: How long have you owned the Raymona Hotel?
A: I don't own the Raymona—I wish I did. *(The tone is arch Ivy League.)* What address? [253 West 49th Street.] Oh, the Ray*mona*. I think we've owned it six to eight months, but it's leased to someone else.
Q: Do you know Jimmy Della Bella?

A: I don't know anybody. The property was purchased because the building is scheduled to be demolished in the next couple of years. We plan to put in a block of office buildings.

Q: How much rent do you get?

A: I don't know.

Q: Is Della Bella the lessee?

A: Why don't you ask him? I've never been inside.

Q: Suppose you were served with an order to close it?

A: So, we'd give it to our attorney to take care of.

Q: Who is your attorney?

A: You're asking too many questions. We have ten properties in New York—all new office and apartment buildings. We don't own anything else like this building. We've gotten a lot of summonses on it and we've done a lot to clean it up.

Q: What have you done exactly?

A: What would *you* do if your face was dirty?

Q: We were discussing the dirt in the Raymona Hotel. You say you have cleaned it up. How do you know if you've never been inside?

A: What do you think this is? I'm a very *very* substantial businessman, and you're asking a lot of stupid questions. I'm not going into that hellhole myself to check the bathrooms. We give the summonses to someone else to take care of. If *you* want to clean up New York, go ahead.

Q: Who takes care of your summonses?

A: I don't know. You find out.

I found out that the attorney for the 50-50 Corporation is Matthew Salko, who happens to be under indictment for allegedly attempting to bribe a cop.

Subsequently, I discovered that this Ivy League landlord had himself been convicted in 1962 on two counts of tax evasion. After Woodner got out of jail, his prosecutor, former U.S. Attorney Robert Morgenthau, subsequently bumped into Woodner at a Mary Lasker party. The guests were being asked to contribute $1,000 each to form a President's Club—they would have a desk at the White House, they could call up anytime with complaints. The first hand up was Ian Woodner's, pledging not $1,000 but $5,000. Morgenthau had to leave the room. He could just imagine Woodner phoning the President to complain about the food at Leavenworth.

Woodner's check was returned the next day.

Oddly, the Lark—the other hotel I had been scrutinizing—appeared nowhere on the original list of prostitution hotels submitted by the Police Department to the mayor's cleanup council. The landowner behind the Lark turned out to be Irving Maidman, a Manhattan real estate magnate for the last half-century, who owns, among other things, a new 100-acre industrial complex on the opposite side of the Hudson; the New York, Susquehanna & Western Railroad Company; and twenty industrial properties on the West Side, including the recently closed West Side Airlines Terminal and the renovated Crossroads Building in the eye of Times Square, where he maintains the family business headquarters. We met there after several phone conversations, and I asked Maidman about the Lark.

"That's not a hotel, that's a joint," said Maidman, quickly explaining that the building is leased to the Riese brothers.

Irving and Murray Riese are a notoriously elusive pair of chain-restaurant owners who chinned up from the East Bronx to their most recent enterprise. They are minority partners in the new Jimmy's Restaurant, successor to the old Toots Shor's, with members of the mayor's inner circle, Richard Aurelio and Sid Davidoff.

"We'd love to get the Rieses out," Mr. Maidman insisted. The Riese brothers pay $25,000-a-year rent, but since they took the net lease for twenty-one years in 1962, the property has been a loser for Maidman, he claimed. Maidman asked his secretary to bring me a copy of the lease. His son Robert, the firm's lawyer, protested.

"We have nothing to hide," said the older Maidman and proceeded with the following tale of woe: He had friends in Loews Theaters Inc. who tipped him off that the Uris brothers were about to put up a giant office building on that block. He talked to the Riese brothers about canceling their lease. No deal. They said they had a lease with the hotel upstairs and would have to compensate them too. "We offered the Riese brothers a substantial sum, $200,000, but they refused to sell the lease at any price. There was only one way they would make a deal—if Uris would promise them a restaurant in his new building. Uris refused." Irving Maidman choked up at this point. "We were going to get almost a *half a million* from the Uris brothers for that building alone—our corner piece was the key."

It stands to reason that if the Riese brothers refused to sell a $25,000 four-story piece of dreck for eight times that amount, somebody is making a profit on the mysterious building on West 50th Street. But I didn't have the pleasure of meeting the Riese brothers for another month.

Irving Maidman is one of the self-made casualties of our flourishing pross and porn industries. At one time he believed Times Square would become the country's finest showcase for legitimate theater. "It didn't happen, so we leased to whom we could." That includes a massage parlor, a live burlesque show, and a number of pornographic movie theaters of which Mr. Maidman professes to be ashamed.

"But you have made a great deal of money," I reminded him.

"It hasn't been easy," he said. "I'm building in St. Croix, I'm over in New Jersey, and in New York my buildings are empty. I've been building up the West Side for fifty years. Now I can't get out fast enough."

His point was well taken. As I left their Times Square headquarters, someone was defecating in the lobby of the Maidman empire.

August 1. Inspector Peterson was furious.

"It's been three-and-a-half months since my task force began operating." He opened his fat arrest file on peep shows, prostitution hotels, massage parlors, live sex shows, licensed and unlicensed porno movie theaters. There were 156 reports. All had the same heading: *Arrest Made In Premises Licensed by the Department of Consumer Affairs.* All had been sent through the chief inspector to Consumer Affairs, recommending they take action. But, as far as the police knew, no action had been taken on any of them.

"Bess Myerson is a sharp piece of work," Peterson said of the former Miss America who has proved to be a formidable adversary as Commissioner of Consumer Affairs, on issues which appeal to her. I heartily agreed. "But she's chasing roaches," Peterson went on. "Everybody's against roaches—but what about the robbery cartels running these massage parlors?"

Now I began to open the drawers of city bureaucracy. The mayor himself had placed major emphasis on the powers of the Consumer Affairs Department to suspend and revoke licenses and to bring injunctive proceedings. In fact, it had more power than all the other city agencies *combined* over these establishments, with the exception of massage parlors. And new legislation had been promised to correct that. Why was Consumer Affairs dragging its feet?

The next day I appeared at the Consumer Affairs Department with copies of the police reports going back to February, and two very simple questions: Who in your office has these reports? Has any action been taken?

Commissioner Myerson was dashing off for California. Bernard Sack, her second deputy commissioner, was packing for Italy. The reports drew blank looks. Did anyone even know of their existence? "Well, if you call Mr. Whosit," "Wait, we'll get Mr. Freedman [the department counsel] to find out."

They could not find out. Finally, Bess, greatly distressed, turned to Sack: "What *are* our legal powers here?"

"Well, the fact is, when pressed to extend our legal jurisdiction we do have limitations. . . ." Et cetera, et cetera. An immensely well-defended civil servant, Bernie Sack drew a large breath and began to lecture me straight from the handbill *Know Your Department of Consumer Affairs*. I said I didn't have time for that, could we move on to the second question. Any action taken?

From the pile of arrest reports I had brought, Bess Myerson drew at random one involving a parking lot operated by Myers Brothers Parking System (the brothers also lease a property assessed at a million dollars on West 47th Street, which houses a peep show). The report described arrests of both a prostitute and the parking lot attendant, who together had offered to arrange "an unlawful act of sexual intercourse with a police officer for $25 and $1 for the use of an auto parked in the lot."

The commissioner's eyes danced. "Let's follow this one up," she said. "This is sexy."

Sack dispatched subdeputies to follow up; more waiting. Finally Bess Myerson turned to Sack and said, "Bernie, *do* we have the power to revoke the licenses in these parking lots where there's prostitution going on in the back of the cars?"

Mr. Sack said, "Well, let's just talk about the legal limitations. . . ." Et cetera, et cetera.

An hour after the commissioner left for California, Bernard Sack conceded icily: "The answer is that I cannot tell you now that we received those *so-called* 156 reports."

August 4. Flat hot afternoon in Hell's Bedroom. The mayor's Code Enforcement Team was waiting for me. Sergeant Sidney Patrick swung open the door of a Midtown North police van and said impatiently, "C'mon, we're hitting massage parlors today and my inspectors leave at three." Abruptly, I was at street level in every sense.

Inspector Chris Bossis from Consumer Affairs asked the police to show me a live peep show on West 42nd Street. "We served them with a summons yesterday, you won't believe it. It's the most degenerate we've ever seen." The sign on the second-floor landing read:

PEEPALIVE—NEW YORK'S ONLY
LIVE PEEP SHOW!
25¢

Inside, Sergeant Patrick quickly shepherded me into one of the twenty black-curtained booths arranged in a circle. Red light on. Performance in progress. I bent to peer through a window the size of a mail slot and there it was—my first peep—a silver-booted black nude spread across a revolving turntable, on her back, manipulating her private parts with consummate boredom, chewing gum. Indeed, had it not been for the gum she would surely have been asleep. Across the way I could see another peeper, the sort of young man one doesn't notice in library stacks. Oh-oh. Word of the raid has passed to the performer. A Puerto Rican child-woman dashes from the dressing room to throw the performer a long chiffon scarf. The shade comes down over my peephole. Show's over. But the most exciting part was still to come. Straightening up, I stepped out of the booth and collided with a menacing employee. He had been behind my back all the while—wielding a golf iron.

"We chased three or four other fellas away from you before him" Chris Bossis said. "Imagine getting in one of these booths here—who's behind you? Putting a knife to you, ready to mug you?

"Wait'll you see the massage parlor upstairs. . . ."

Undoubtedly, Peepalive, Roman Massage Parlor, Rector Books and Bob's Bargain Books—the whole layer cake—was the most degenerate pornographic assemblage in the City of New York. They are all owned by corporations, the principal officer or attorney for which is Edward R. Finch II, the uncle of Edward

Finch Cox—President Nixon's son-in-law.

Edward R. Finch is also the son of a deceased New York State Appellate Court Judge, whose venerated likeness hangs in the son's office on 44th Street and to whom he refers deferentially as "the judge." The phone conversation I later had with Finch was the shortest of all exchanges with the landlords of Hell's Bedroom:

"I don't own any buildings on 42nd."

"You are saying you do not own 105, 107 and 109 West 42nd?"

"I do not. Your information is completely erroneous."

"Your name is listed as the principal of the Finch Corporation, which is listed as the owner of 105—"

Mr. Finch broke in, voice taut as wire: "I do not own those buildings. Look, we're a law firm. There are managing agents who take care of all that. Look, I have people here in my office."

He hung up.

One name among the major landlords of Hell's Bedroom was known, yet had remained unscathed. He was, after all, the largest land assembler in midtown and a vocal member of the mayor's Times Square Development Council. Yet, on closer study, Seymour Durst showed two faces. One face was basking in the glow of praise he had heaped upon himself for closing two of his prostitution hotels. (By my count, that left four to go.) The other face was making deals as usual.

Hypocrisy should be made of sterner stuff. When pressed, the mask of good intentions slipped. "When we closed down the Aristo Hotel," Durst told me, "we were able to get higher income from the stores on Forty-fourth Street." As a public relations gesture,

Durst tried to give away the vermin-ridden Aristo as a youth hostel. "We liked the idea of changing from hustling to hosteling," he said, "but they told us it would cost too much to put into condition." What Durst failed to mention, until pressed, was his continuing ownership of two bookstores and four pornographic movie houses—the Love, Pix, and Avon, all on West 42nd Street, and the Avon-Hudson on West 44th—which together pull in annual rents of close to a half million dollars. "I don't think these porn theaters are going to get out," he told me. There is no substitute use for the property except parking lots, he explained. "And these theaters bring in considerably higher rents than we could get for parking."

Durst's activities clearly demonstrated that when the landlords of Hell's Bedroom plead helplessness, they are lying through their receipts.

August 14. On the peep show front, Kassner and Detsky brought suit against the city on behalf of the group of peeps owned by Marty Hodas, the Mafia-connected porno entrepreneur. The charge was "Gestapo tactics" when police went on a three-day drive against peep shows, padlocking coin boxes and arresting the front-counter flunkies again. A gentleman's agreement was reached between the city and the peep-show exhibitors—who vigorously object to appearing in court even to pursue their own injunctions, since they must leave their fingerprints behind. Pending Supreme Court decisions, the cops would cool arrests if Hodas and his crew agreed to show only softporn films.

Jumping ahead here—just to show how long nothing can happen while something seems to be—focus on Monday, October 16, 1972: the Supreme Court finally confronted the massage parlor issue. It upheld a Virginia State courts law banning massages by members of the opposite sex. That meant every municipality could now pass an ordinance outlawing intersexual massages.

"Now the blood will flow and heads will roll in midtown," predicted a weary but triumphant assistant corporation counsel, Michael Klein.

"No chance," the inimitable Kassner and Detsky had already vowed. "We're just going to take down the Body Rub signs [their last gimmick, designed to defeat the mayor's legislation requiring both the massage parlors and their employees to be licensed]. And we're just going to put up signs saying Nude Photo Modeling."

The next day, October 17, was enough to drive any corporation counsel to drink. The peep-show exhibitors had been hurting financially. Their public demanded hard-core. And so they breached the agreement with the city and gave pubic hair back to their public.

Michael Klein phoned Herman Tarnow, civilian legal adviser to the Third Division of police, all in a flap. "They're showing hard-core again, Herman."

"I know, I'm out in the street looking at the films billed right now," Tarnow said, but with no urgency in his voice.

"Herman, get your men out there!" Klein cheered. "Bust 'em. Kill 'em!"

"Look, we're short on money," said Herman Tarnow, servant of a city with a $9 billion budget doing face-to-face combat with indicted members of the Mafia-financed midtown pornography industry. "We're trying to get $100 in quarters to give the men to see the shows."

Assistant Corporation Counsel Michael Klein (salary $13,500) had seen the pitfalls of the mayor's multiagency task force early that summer. He had suggested it be led by two assistant corporation counsels and, like Inspector Peterson, predicted all would be in vain if the cases did not end up before a coordinated panel of judges. His insights were ignored. By mid-August, the Corporation Counsel's office finally was brought into the battle. Israel Rubin, chief of the Penalties Division, discovered a statute in the Public Health Law never before used against prostitution hotels. Frustrated to the point of fight or flee, Michael Klein stayed up all night writing the first brief so the city would move before another summer went to waste.

The Hotel Raymona was selected for the test case. Movement began at last. . . .

August 24. The process server hits the Raymona at 5:00 P.M. Jimmy Della Bella is busy taking a bet from Dedsrolz, a welfare case with an angry knob of cancer on his eyelid.

"Did I get any food stamps today?"

"Yeah, but you better not vote for Lindsay this year," Della Bella says. "You won't get no raise."

Dedsrolz gives a thin whiskey laugh. "Gotta get some money so I can get this thing taken off my eye. I dunno, tumor maybe. It's got veins in it."

Enter the process server. "I'm from the Corporation Counsel's office. I have here an order to show cause against the Hotel Raymona, the 50-50 Corporation, and Security National Bank."

"I dunno nuthin' about nuthin'," Della Bella yawns. "I just work here."

"Is your name James Della Bella?"

Drop-jawed: "You have *my* name too?"

Scowling, Della Bella scans the document and its two-page arrest record. He is ordered to cease and desist from operating the hotel as a public nuisance. A flunky reports that the process server is taping a copy to the downstairs door.

In defiant contempt of court, Jimmy swipes the order off his door. While two curious beat officers read over his shoulder, he shakes a prophetic fist at the sky: "We'll be here next year and the year after and the year after that. The *Church* will go before we go!"

One of the gumshoes, oblivious, steps aside to let Twinky Bizi through with a trick. "You know," says the cop, "I think he's right."

On their first inspection of the Hotel Cleo at Eighth Avenue and 55th Street, Inspector Peterson's task force made a gun collar and found one toilet for fifty-six rooms. The leaseholders are two Hasidim, Kabeck and Binda of BTF Realty Corporation. The tenants are a beaten lot of gaunt, black, tubercular welfare cases. A vacate order was posted by the Rent and Housing Maintenance Department, which led Midtown North Captain Joseph Flynn to remark, "Sometimes you hate what you have to do as a cop."

A week later A.C.C. Michael Klein brought an action against the Radio Center Hotel, which reeked with muggings, stabbings, dope, grand and petit larceny arrests, plus thirty-eight prostitution arrests and twelve convictions since January 1971. Here the owner is a client of William Klein II, a Park Avenue attorney. Klein seemingly cooperated fully with the city, having been unsuccessful in attempts to clean up the premises after two years of legal efforts on his own. He changed the management. But on October 26th, the last time I visited the Radio Center, it was still in action as a prostitution hotel. The operator, a gregarious middle-aged black woman, explained: "I come with the building."

Next on Michael Klein's list was the Hotel Somerset, whose lessee was Max Shaub. Called to task by Inspector Peterson, he promised to turn it into a welfare hotel.

"It's a steadier buck," he said.

September 24. The Hotel Lark was on Michael Klein's hit list at last.

The fun began when the process server set out to find the Riese brothers. Their lease with Irving Maidman was held in the name of 830 Restaurant, Inc., at 883 Sixth Avenue. "Wonder why they have a corporation called 830 Restaurant at an address like 883?" puzzled the process server. "It's so confusing."

"That's the point of the game," I suggested. In two months of tracking I had not been able to come up with a company name for the Riese brothers, much less an address. Irving Maidman said he couldn't keep up with them. Former Mayor Robert Wagner was foggy about their whereabouts, though it was during his administration that the Riese brothers, in their own words, "went to the moon."

Today they own the Child's chain, the Cobb's Corner chain, the Calico Kitchen chain, the Brewery chain, a beehive of hamburger joints one class up from counter service known as Burger & Brew, and the hot dog concession on the Staten Island Ferry. And—controlling interest in Longchamps at four locations, and the Autopub on Fifth Avenue, and nine concessions in Grand Central Station, and the 900-seat Riverboat restaurant in the Empire State Building, and what the Riese brothers call "our *class* restaurants": Lüchow's, Steer Palace and the brand-new Chicago on Park Avenue. Most recently, they have leased 13,500 square feet of retail space in the concourse of One Penn Plaza at a cost of $7 million, where they plan to open three or four more restaurants. More: they have leased the main-floor dining facilities in the Roosevelt Hotel on Madison Avenue for twenty-five years, for $3 million aggregate rent plus a percentage of the business.

Their offices at 883 Sixth Avenue turned out to be an Executive Billiard Parlor.

The Assistant Corporation Counsel suggested we try another address, a block from the Lark on 50th Street, which is a Cobb's Corner heavily patronized by prostitutes on their coffee break. The cashier, a newly hired Italian grandpa, assumed we were trying to sell advertising. He showed us the card given him by a hiring boss named Ronnie Dunkley: National Restaurants at 1491 Broadway. "A very clever man," he described Dunkley, "colored fellow, but educated."

The front office for National Restaurants, appropriately, was a Child's Ham 'n' Eggs in the heart of Times Square. The mezzanine level held a clutter of desks and file cabinets. A waiter demanded we come down. We asked for Irving Riese. He howled with laughter.

"Oh no, we never see Mr. Riese."

A great pillow of an Italian-American man sat at the table closest to the cash register, answering a five-line push-button phone and telling callers Mr. Dunkley wasn't in. At six, the employees bristled, "Here he comes."

Suave, orchid-shirted, bedecked with a jeweled

stickpin and gold I.D. bracelet, Ronnie Dunkley went straight to the register and nimbly counted the cash. Too late to serve the show-cause order, the process server had left for the day.

I suggested to the photographer that we wander over to Jimmy's restaurant and see what we could see. We followed Dick Aurelio into the dim New Yorkese bar, bumped into his partner Sid Davidoff and asked for Irving Riese.

"He's right behind you," Davidoff said.

Irving Riese is the size of a jockey. His face recedes, his teeth are small, his head dips obsequiously during conversation. One struggles to find in his all-over grayishness a memorable characteristic, until he explains his style.

"We've always shied away from publicity, but you must understand why. We don't want the world to know the Riese brothers hold the Staten Island Ferry concession *and* Steer Palace—they might think our steaks and hot dogs are from the same meat!"

But there is another reason for their "shyness," which is also the secret of the Riese brothers' success. "It's called the shell corporation," whispers Irving Riese. He orders us a bottle of wine, a steak for himself, and agrees reluctantly to sit down and explain. "If a corporation breaks a lease and declares bankruptcy, the bank can go after its other assets. *Unless* it has no other assets." His tiny teeth flash in a smile brief as a shuffle of cards. "And that is why the Riese brothers make a new corporation for every restaurant lease!" He estimates they own 150 different corporations at this point (of which 830 Restaurant, Inc. is a droplet in the bucket).

Of course, one suddenly gets the point of this man's all-over grayishness! For fifty-three years Irving Riese has cultivated the unobtrusiveness of a ferret. He describes himself as a moving target, ever on the prowl from one chain to another, checking the proportions of whiskey to mix, brew to burger, teetotalers to dipsomaniacs at the $10.95 all-you-can-drink retirement dinners which pack his Riverboat restaurant. Where Irving cannot be in the flesh, he monitors by phone. All over town the help is on alert for his calls, at midnight, two, four in the morning; his home telephone is connected by special lines to every restaurant in his chains.

Before asking directly about his income from the Lark Hotel, I warm up by asking Irving Riese why he is a partner in Jimmy's. He says with pride that Jimmy's is the only restaurant in which the Riese brothers are silent "but Murray will tell you all about the business side." Murray is the younger half of the Riese brothers. Irving must go now. Can we meet again? Next week at Lüchow's, he says.

I stopped to ask Dick Aurelio about his new partners on the way out. "I could tell you a lot about the Riese brothers," he said, adding nervously, "not all of it good." How then did he happen to know them? "You can't run the City of New York and miss the Riese brothers." And his sudden interest in the restaurant business? "The day after the campaign folded [and Lindsay lost his bid for the White House], Sid Davidoff came to me and said, 'What're we going to do now?' We gave ourselves overnight to come up with an idea. Sid came back with the restaurant business. I said, 'What do we know about the *restaurant* business?' So I went to the experts—and here we are with Jimmy's!"

Mayor Lindsay's latest and greatest midtown cleanup was eight months old. I thought it odd that his chief political aide and former deputy mayor was in partnership with the proprietors of one of the prime targets of his war on prostitution.

When I saw the brothers Riese together at Lüchow's, Murray, the deal maker, did most of the talking. He claims they have owned a thousand leases in their lives and have rarely sold one back. "You might as well tell my brother to sell one of his children. He's in *love* with his restaurants."

And finally we talked about the deterioration of midtown. The next mayor must be a strong law-enforcement man, said the brothers, that's the first thing. "I don't think the prostitutes are bad, but if a man is going to go with a prostitute and get mugged, that's bad." Precisely what the Rieses of this city have always said: it's the mayor's fault, the prostitute's fault, the police department's fault, never *their* fault.

I asked them to be specific. Did they have any properties where prostitution hotels, peep shows, massage parlors, or porno movie houses were tenants?

"Yeah, but you see what can happen—" and Murray gave his version of how landlords can be trapped by pornography tenants. "Should *I* decide because I think *Playboy* is pornographic, I will not sell it on my newsstand? If somebody *tells* me it's pornographic, and it's against the *law* for me to sell it, I won't sell it. Now if you want to know if we own a massage parlor or a peep show or a pornographic bookstore, the answer is absolutely, unequivocally no. Never have owned one, never will own one—"

"You visit your restaurants all the time," I interrupted. "Surely you must have noticed the Lark Hotel. It has been operating above your restaurant at 830 Eighth Avenue since *before* you leased the property in October 1962."

"Do I know that's a fleabag hotel without even going up there? Yes. But when we took over the property, you could get all the people in a rodeo in Madison Square Garden to go into that hotel," Murray said.

"And our restaurant downstairs was a grrrrrrreat restaurant," Irving added.

"Surely you weren't depending on business from the Garden," I said. "It was announced in 1960, two years before you leased the building, that a new Garden was going up."

Murray said the Riese brothers never believe until they see.

I asked if they didn't recall an offer from Irving Maidman to buy their lease *after* 1962?

Blank looks. Ah yes, then the recollection.

"All he had to do was make me an offer," Irving Riese said.

"He says he offered you $200,000," I said.

We went back and forth with that one for a while and finally Irving Riese said he figures that Irving Maidman could never make a deal with the Uris Brothers.

"Now we're waiting for the Uris Building to fill up. Then our Burger & Brew [beneath the Lark Hotel] will do much more business." Irving swiftly moved the conversation in the direction of their newest chain, Burger & Brew: "It's going to be a colossus. At this moment we have five, by the end of this year we'll build *thirty*. That's the way the Riese brothers think!"

Murray, who never finished high school, said it's a real rags-to-riches story. "We decided very early in life, we've worked our guts out for our money and nobody's going to take our profits away from us. We went into business when I was sixteen. We were both working as dishwashers for 35 cents an hour at Krum's [a large candy store and ice-cream parlor] and living on Bathgate Avenue in the Bronx. My brother was courting his first wife. She gave him a lumber jacket for his birthday. He took it back to Davega's in Times Square and got the $24. I organized a strike at Krum's and when the state awarded me $400 in back pay, that was the $424 we used to buy our first luncheonette!" They expanded that business into the first cart service, hustling offices in the RCA Building, until one day Irving said to Murray, "Let's sell restaurants instead of sandwiches." They proceeded to buy cafeterias, luncheonettes, nightclubs, frankfurter stands, drugstores, and finally, in 1961, their first "big" buy—$2.5 million with a $500,000 cash payment—the Child's Restaurant Company. Where did they get a half million in cash?

"We borrowed it! From the bread man, the coffee man, the linen man. Oh man, do you know how much coffee—I'd say we give our supplier $10 million worth of coffee business a year," said Murray, who is a cannibal when it comes to buying restaurants. Food turns him off; he eats hot dogs three times a week. But when describing how he negotiates a deal, he literally salivates: "The game all begins in negotiating the lease, now you have an adversary, eyeball-to-eyeball contact. And the minute that deal is made, I'm off looking for a new purchase; a philanderer—I always need a new 'girl.'"

Today the Riese brothers employ 3,500 people and have an annual payroll of $13 million. No parent company. No board of directors. No stockholders. Only an "inner cabinet" composed of accountant Larry Abrams, construction man Barney Goldman, and top kitchen man Eamon Doland, formerly a captain in the Irish Army, of whom Murray says they are very proud. Still a gunslinger at heart, Doland must be gently reminded that America has such things as unions.

"Now I come to the part I'm most proud of about the Riese brothers," Murray said. "We share *everything*. One bank account, one signature, there's no accounting between the Riese brothers."

Irving Riese stood up with a final flourish. "We're the fiftieth largest feeders in the world!"

They drove off into the night, two little kings in a long black limousine.

October 2. Midnight. Chilly. Shades were drawn on the Raymona Hotel. The reflector was dull. The game, according to the mayor's office, was almost over. But as I drove past, from habit, I turned around for a last glimpse of that infamous windowed door.

A face, a witch, a ravaged and terrible retread of a face, rose up from the shadows. There was a flicker of white elephant earrings. Minnesota Marsha grinned.

Final Score. Inspector Peterson sent to his superior in September a report on the state of his command.

On the state of prostitution he wrote: "It remains a constant problem. Cooperation from the courts is needed in this area. . . . Prostitutes are released from court and frequently re-arrested on the same day. The solution has not been reached due to the District Attorney's refusal to prosecute for this violation. Prostitutes have the impression the arrests are just part of the working conditions."

On crime in the center of Hell's Bedroom: "The assignment of foot patrols on a steady basis has dramatically reduced the incidence of violent crime."

On the state of Eighth Avenue: "This area is still considered a problem area of the command. Cheap hotels and rooming houses attract addicts and prostitutes. Narcotics is heavy."

On impact on the public: "Residents report added foot patrols do give a feeling of added protection. Businessmen in the community feel increased police patrols have helped, but have pushed the undesirables off the street and into their premises."

In conclusion, the inspector pleaded that the extra three hundred men assigned to his command not be recalled—which could happen at any time. "If they take back my men," he told me, "the wave we've been fighting back for the last eight months will roll over us again—in a month!"

—In October the Inspector "took back his sidewalk." That is, every night at eight he throws up police barricades on the sidewalks along the west side of Eighth Avenue from 45th to 49th streets, creating a gauntlet close to the buildings which the pimps must walk. "I told them to make it two pimps wide." To enforce the gauntlet, he formed what his men called the Goon Squad—ten of the biggest cops he could find. Now when the pimps walk past, all the Goons have to say is, "You betta not stop, mutha." It's something.

—Deputy Mayor Edward K. Hamilton, at a dinner party in late October, confidently pronounced, "The midtown cleanup is happening."

—This reporter certified, on a walking tour in late October, that all twelve prostitution hotels in Midtown North—despite the show-cause orders issued against six of them, despite a few changes of names in management and court hearings in various stages of postponement by Kassner and Detsky—were all operating with business as usual.

—Sergeant Patrick of Midtown North reported in

October: "We started with sixteen massage parlors back in April. Now we have twenty-five. And more opening every week." One owner plans to spend $35,-000 to decorate his newest massage parlor. He has promised to send Sergeant Patrick an invitation to his opening cocktail party.

The prostitutes continue to take all the arrests, the police to suffer frustration, the lawyers to mine gold, the operators to laugh, the landowners to insist they have no responsibility, the mayor to issue press releases. The nature of the beast is, in a word, greed.

Standing back from this open-air asylum with its cast of thousands, there is only one possible conclusion. Somebody out there does not want Hell's Bedroom cleaned up. And he's serving champagne.

Chapter Six

"Nobody being hustled believes it." The
hustler of that motto began as a double-
talking Bronx boy and now finds himself exiled in Bernard Cornfeld's château
in the French Alps. His hasty exit from the
United States in June 1972 was forced by five
felony counts on which he was indicted by a
Los Angeles County Grand Jury. His play-
mates this time were a senator's son, a
Playboy bunny and a drug called MDA. But
his reputation was made before all that in
the penthouses of Manhattan's upper East
Side, where he will always be remembered
as that twenty-four-hour worldbeater . . .

DAVID THE PIMP

The meaty blonde girl, stiffened in apparent terror,
backs across the doorway of the beauty salon—a whip
parts the air close as a zipper to her side and smacks
the floor.

"Heel!" a voice commands.

Heads flip out of their speed-dryer plugs; everyone in
the beauty salon turns toward the brutal scene. No-
ooo, the girl moans. Her attacker comes into view: he
is young, Caucasian, and sucked-out lean. His face
resembles the hood ornament on an old Pontiac.
Gloved in a brown suede Western suit, he is brandish-
ing a leather belt with a horse-bit buckle. Again he
arches like a matador and—*swock*—brings down his
belt within millimeters of the girl's flesh.

"I said heel!"

The girl giggles.

"That's him," the salon owner proudly announces to his flock. "That's David, the second-greatest pimp in New York."

Of course the clientele has been titillated through endless Balsam rinses by tales of David the Pimp, the stunts he pulls among the rich, the outrageous artistry of his double-talk, the baffling power he wields over young beauties despite the fact that he exploits them, degrades them and generally has no personal sexual use for them. The salon owner has several purposes in relating such tales. In the first place, conventional East Side wives at the spreading-thighs stage of life are far better entertained by perversity than politics. Second, the salon owner is in awe of David the Pimp— would that *he* had such nerve. Finally, the arrangement. David sends his new girls to the salon for an introductory rinse, trim, styling and pedicure; the salon owner in turn softens up possible customers for David by building the expectations of his clients toward the day when they will see, with their own eyes, the second-greatest pimp in New York. This is it!

"Listen to me," David begins, laughing as he enters at the success of his own David the Pimp act. A brief distraction while he fondles the breasts of the girl with him—"Ah, the ecstasies we have known together this day"—and then he delves into her handbag.

"Say hello to my girl friend Karen, she's just back from excavating in British Honduras with three cases full of pre-Columbian art and an ocelot. All right, ladies, get your tapestries while you can! He dances from chair to chair with bolts of exotic cloth over his arm, a suede pouch bulging with scarab rings in one hand, and in the other, mud bowls. "A lot of broken bowls to you perhaps, but worth $18,000. And this ivory, *this ivory*"—he dangles a tusk before a blue-tinted lady who gasps with delight—"you know the girl in Woolworth's who says, 'Thank you for your purchases'? This ivory is a chip from her tooth."

At this point a nineteen-year-old actress, gifted with the evanescent beauty of a green apple, sits up from her shampoo. She looks once, shyly, at the man making all this commotion. Then she turns away in the manner of well-bred single girls caught staring in hotel lobbies.

David the Pimp hoists his spatulate hips and sets his legs in the arched-bow position, which all hustlers learn from watching TV Westerns. He swaggers over to her.

"I warn you, I'm a bastard / a brute / a guy who buys nothing, but takes it / a deceitful motherfucker / a person who has no respect for any other individual / a disgusting degenerate human being. Now—," David bends close, "would you like me to pick you up?"

The actress laughs. Her voice says no, I have a boy friend, my director, but her eyes say yes, this is better than Jack Nicholson in *Five Easy Pieces*.

"Is your boy friend beautiful?" David demands. "Good, I can't stand ugly people around me. Bring your boy friend too. Tonight we are going to have a party you will not believe, my $1000-a-pound grass, my château wine $30 a bottle. I've got the thirteenth-richest man in America coming." Pause. "You think I'm handsome?"

"Sort of," the actress says.

"*Sort of.* Paul, bring me a dryer." David leans intensely toward the mirror. He wets, brushes and fluff-dries his hair, curling it into perfect commas over the shoulders of his custom-made suede suit (fabric stolen from Macy's), and then he wets, brushes and fluffs it dry again. "Paul, it needs straightening," he decides. "I looked terrible Saturday night."

"How old are you?" the actress asks.

"Guess."

"Twenty-six."

"Exacta*mente*. Now I guess. Thirty-four C."

"How did you—"

"I'm in the anatomy business, my dear."

(The salon owner has already informed his flock of David's latest credit. He was "technical adviser" for Jane Fonda on the Warner Brothers film *Klute*, in which she plays a Manhattan call girl.)

The archaeologist, pouting slightly, slips an arm around David from behind. He drops another warning (enticement) to the actress: "You know, I am outrageously well endowed."

And now a final flourish, the line that causes all manner of unexpected lovelies to decide this man must be saved, and that they alone can transform him from unsated profligate to contented lover: "Will you tell me why God gave me the greatest sexual equipment in the world and all my girl friends are lesbians?"

That's it. The ten-minute hustle. David gathers up his tapestries, bowls, suede fringe bags, seventy dollars in cash and his archaeologist, and blows a kiss to the actress. Gone.

"Where's your party?" the actress calls.

David smiles, triumphant.

He backbends across the doorway and gives an address in the East 70s. "And bring your beautiful boy friend. Penthouse H—H for hooker."

Thus at 5:00 P.M. on a Thursday afternoon David the Pimp slides into his hemlock-green limousine a happy man, having launched another night and day in the life of the twenty-four-hour worldbeater. From here he will repair to Yonkers Raceway. The money will be squandered on one race, but his very abandon will attract people. More people. Then he will come back and give a grand party for them all in his penthouse. Every 24 hours David repeats the same cycle.

It is only fitting that such a naturally gifted con artist should ply his trade on the upper East Side of Manhattan. This is the province of Let's Pretend located in the state of Anomie. Here people's lives touch by chance encounter, or by an exchange of coin in the laundry room. Here daddy's girls stalk the wild asparagus before their youth runs out and the pleasant handyman hangs the stewardess's blinds before raping her. It is the natural habitat of the *haut monde* of pimps.

Hustlers observe the subtleties of marginal differentiation more slavishly than any group of Wall Street lawyers; they are snobs. In a splurge of modesty David will admit to being only the second-greatest pimp of his class, but that class is exclusively inhabited by those who do business with the rich by telephone. For street pimps they have nothing but contempt.

The present titleholder of first-greatest pimp, according to David, is Charlie. He lives in the same building as David but manages a stable of professional hookers with calloused hips who lack, by David's standards, certain social graces. Charlie is black, pimping being by and large a black business. The very fact that David, a skinny Jewish kid from Taft High School, overcame his handicaps to become the *second greatest* of his class—well, why quibble in the winner's circle?

David's life is kinetic art, the art of the realm. Much as Henry Ford must have sensed the fortune to be made in satisfying the compulsion of his era for personal speed, so David as a boy hustler in the sexually retarded fifties sensed that the profit of his age was to be made in slaking the most infernal thirsts of the flesh.

He was in business with his first hooker at the age of fifteen. Ellen was her name; she was the one natural nyphomaniac in the class, an assessment David was able to make immediately upon entering Taft High School. At the time he was lodging at Ames Pool Hall, 44th Street off Sixth Avenue, having been thrown out of twelve schools and his home in the Bronx. (Ames provided a particularly inspirational home life: *The Hustler* was being filmed there.) He took Ellen to the track and introduced her to thirty-five-year-old horse-players. She took them back to her parents' house, for which David rewarded her in the currency most highly valued by her peers: clothes (stolen). "Ellen was the best-dressed girl in high school," he insists.

Meanwhile, David spotted a new lifeline in the race-track. Indeed, it was the "Carlotta caper" which earned him his majority in the criminal world.

Everyone has financial problems, even biology teachers. David was only too happy to match his biology teacher's fifty to a winning horse each week. Word spread among the faculty that the boy was a tactical wizard. He also built a spotless reputation: David always gave credit, always paid off. One must be reliable while building toward the score of scores.

One day David put out a call for seed money from every student and teacher in his network. He left school with $4,100. Carlotta was a long shot, but he bet the wad on Carlotta. She paid $34.80. Somehow, with over $65,000 in his pocket, the skinny kid from Ames Pool Hall could not bring himself to go back to school.

A month later, in Miami, where he was busily engaged in buying a $125,000 apartment house with a phony check and hookers for collateral, David received a gift from one of his old friends in the Taft High School shop class. It was a T-square engraved simply: *Carlotta, 1961*.

"So I should never forget." He says it with genuine reverence.

Today, at twenty-six, David has moved well beyond biology teachers. He exploits the exploiters—the conglomerate directors, the electronic comedians and slick publishers, concentrating particularly on those six-figure patrons of the arts who are denied the standing of aristocrats, having made their money ignobly and too fast. America specializes in such social casualties, all those little boys with Erector Sets grown big who build museums and pleasure islands and triplexes to themselves, and then discover they have no one to put in them.

Ring David. Penthouse H—H for hooker.

Be warned. David is the juggler, always balancing the forces of will and desire, your volition against his manipulation, working out the combinations of weakness in those around him which can best be coupled, or tripled, or grouped, until their bodies become his possession. Fear no evil for David is your shepherd, you shall not want. He makes it all seem—so natural.

David can think of more ways to extract money in less time than a ball takes to arc the juggler's head. He sells his girls, sells tips on the horses, and he pays all his bills with his women. In a good month $20,000 may pass through his hands. Yet a newcomer to David's circle will notice that, curiously, the pimp never seems to have much cash. Indeed, in the beginning he may refuse payment from his most wealthy Johns. Why? Because he relishes their *obligation* to him. Rich men can always be tapped for a bigger score later on; meanwhile, their obligation proves to David that he is needed, he exists. Money in the bank, what is that? This man loves the challenge of making a hustle minute by minute, scoring a wad and blowing it all at the track and coming back to what he is and always will be: a hustler whose elaborate life style keeps people hanging around just to see what happens next.

David never says hello. This is the cornerstone of his success. He *begins* four beats ahead with some outrageous remark and from there he goes. His artistry is double-talk. Boast, gush, promise, pontificate, gabble, whiffle, yammer, rant—what did he say? The point is to attract attention. Leave them laughing, but confused. This could work only for a white hustler. The black hustler's very life depends on his ability to make a keen, on-the-spot assessment of human character. Not talk. Excessive talk would only attract attention to himself, and for a black man that is always dangerous.

But for David the Pimp, the more vulgar his presentation, the more outlandishly obvious his hustle, the more loudly he strips away our cultural illusions by taking the part of the clown—the harder they laugh.

Tell them what a hustler you are, David.

"I'm a worldbeater, the laughing man, I'm a hope ship to fifty men in this town. I have the richest women for my hookers. The richest. With me they're sluts. I have the greatest freaks of all as my Johns. Everybody that's somebody owes me. Everybody. When they're with me, on my time, they're *with me,* because I take them out of their everyday business and verbal occurrence."

But you say you're a "good guy" hustler.

"Of course. I always let the guy cut his own throat. They beg me to hustle them. The whole world is masochist. A man comes to me with his weakness. I magnify it to an immense portion of his body. Ten times a day on the phone I throw it up to him until I take over his mind. I take over his moment of ecstasy. In my world the castrated man is made a man. The best is when I meet thirty new guys in one month and they give me $2,500 each.

"The figure isn't important. What's important is, they all think I'm their guy, alone!"

Tell again, David, how the money sifts through your fingers.

"Life is a horse race. There has to be one winner, in the sense of a winner being a rich man. That's it. That's bread. I love it. And I do everything I want. I robbed Rye Beach Playland for $13,800 when I was seventeen, so you can imagine where my mind is."

You have so many girls—do you enjoy making love?

"Do you have any idea how many naked breasts I see in a week? My girls are all over me, they just want to screw with me. I hate it. But I gotta take care of them. *I'm* the prostitute. God knows the bills I get from the hotels in San Juan for payoffs on prostitution busts. They're my daughters. The only time I enjoy sex is when I'm doing it for money. I'm the best in my business because I hate it so much."

Your parents were affluent. Do you hate them?

"Please, I do not hate my parents. I hate my *grandparents* for having them. My parents own a monster electrical firm and they make millions of dollars and I don't want it. *I don't want it!* I want to get me and my slaves and Spartacus and get the hell outta here!"

But you are out. You are free, isn't that right?

"Free? I'm so advanced in my thinking that as soon as I'm on a road someplace my head is already back."

But now it is Thursday and from here, who can say? Every twenty-four hours this hustler goes for googol, the score of scores. Pronounce it gooo-gul. Mathematical infinity. A number that is equal to one followed by 100 zeroes.

$$10^{10^{10^{10}}}$$

That's right. That's it. That's googol!

11:00 P.M., same night.

The actress steps uncertainly into the elevator and presses David's floor. It is one of those anonymous brick pillboxes in the East 70s where the elevator is scarred from perpetually moving furniture. The actress's boy friend, a director with deckle-edged silver hair, is impeccably robed in Park Avenue dinner clothes. He plays nervously with his shirt ruffles.

"He's the funniest pimp, really, I just want you to meet him," the actress encourages her unenthusiastic boy friend.

"Will we have to *do* anything?"

"Oh no, we'll just watch."

A young flunky opens the door to an eclectic Casbah: fluming pampas plumes, ferns, feathers, peacock eyes, and waxen tropical foliage hover over long, low banquettes covered with Indian throws and Greek pillows. Everything is bathed in a bluewobble glow from the single headlight which revolves in the ceiling. Incense stings the nose. Difficult to see—there's David on the kitchen phone, 117 pounds naked to the waist. He waves the couple into the main room. A mirrored coffee table is surrounded by four bloated beanbags covered in red plastic, apparently designed for seductive floor-sitting. The only occupant is a small Scottie dog.

"The actress, right?" David jolts into the room buttoning his jeans.

"Right, and this is—" the actress, unable to think of a false name, waves in the direction of her boy friend. He remains posed like an ad for After-Six formal wear.

David smacks his forehead: "What is this, bridge and whist time?"

The director formally extends his hand. "Hello, I'm Jonas." At the same time the actress comes up with, "This is Tom."

"Terrific, Tom, you are an elegant man. Sit down and make yourself at home. We've got a great show for you tonight. Three of the most beautiful hookers in New York coming up, all $500-a-night girls. Hey, where should I put these plumes to give them highlights?" David darts about the room rearranging his Occidental hothouse while continuing, like a circus barker, to arouse his audience. "I've got another girl coming over, very rich, very sick girl. She gets $1,700 a month allowance from her father, a Wall Street tycoon. This August she turns twenty-one and comes into $3 million, if her divorce is out of the way."

"How do you know her?" the actress asks.

"Aha, this girl has a heart of gold. She rents limousines for all her friends. Thousands of dollars of limousine bills she has, but she doesn't want papa to know, understand? So she came to me. They all come to me. So I taught her how to hook."

David brings on his $1,000-a-pound Colombian grass and a dusty bottle of wine, unlabeled. "They bring it over for me sixty bottles at a time on a special boat from France."

The telephone rings. David leaps to the kitchen: "Hello, Virginia darling." There must be two hundred girls listed by their first names in the battered address book beside the kitchen phone, but each one is greeted as if her little fits and starts were David's exclusive concern.

"Virginia," he instructs, "understand this about your husband and his crowd. You're nothing but an ornament. A beautiful meaningless ornament all done up in silver foil. They take you to a club, show you off, but they don't give a damn for you, Virginia. I'm your friend. I can get your apartment paid for. I'll get my junketeer to put up the $600. I'll put *my* friendship with *my* junketeer on the line. For you, Virginia."

Virginia says she is sticking with David all the way. He gives her the address of a gentle flagellant who wants a steady girl.

The telephone rings. This time it's a fabled art collector with a Lolita fixation. "Of course I have a little daughter for you." David dials Diana and tells her to talk like she's fourteen and then brings the two together on his conference phone. On this wondrous instrument it is possible to dial two outside parties and connect them on the same call. David also moves freely between extensions in his kitchen, bedroom, and bathroom, since he sometimes finds it necessary to talk to six people at once. His monthly telephone bill averages $400. Con Ed he cheats blind but the telephone company he pays with pleasure. Like all egoists he cannot bear to be alone, hence the constant flow of girls through his penthouse and the automatic fire of phone calls, none of which he refuses. His conference phone is his greatest pleasure. Its wires are his extremities, sweeping the bottom of the city like pool snakes, sucking in all manner of flotsam and jetsam—and, with luck, the lost diamond rings and gold teeth.

Oblivious to his guests, the pimp is now totally absorbed in receiving orders from his Johns and dispatching his girls.

"Listen to me, Valentino," he can be heard enthusing, "I've got a very good deal for you. You're invited to a 150-foot yacht party, Baron bla bla of bla bla [he gives the name of the well-known chief executive of a major American conglomerate], multimillionaire, one o'clock tomorrow at the 79th Street boat basin. Valentino, you're the best in my stable, I mean it. I need that beautiful tan you brought back from Greece."

David returns finally to his guests. The actress is flipping; does he really know Baron bla bla? Know him! David puts the actress on his bathroom extension and dials Westchester.

"Hello, Baron? Listen to me, I want to ask you a question. How big is your yacht? A hundred feet, okay, how many men are going to be on this boat? Okay, I'm giving all the girls what is known as MDA, Spanish fly to you. When they attack—now this is not a laughing matter—they're gonna be like jackrabbits, you understand? All right, now this is the message I want to impart: Keep the crew members down in the pit. [Gurgling laughter can be heard on the other end.] Got that, Baron? *Keep the crew members in the pit.*"

The actress is suitably impressed. But there is trouble here in Penthouse H.

12:30 A.M. Friday already, and none of his big Johns have turned up for the party. Now two girls of distinctly different types appear at the door. The one in a brief wetsuit, a pro by the looks of her pouting stomach, glances suspiciously about the room. "Okay, where are they?"

David ignores her and ushers in what looks like a thoroughbred Park Avenue beauty. Frightened eyes, that is the first thing one notices. Dressed in an antique velvet jacket and long skirt over Biba boots, with strong brown hair gushing over her shoulders, she calls to mind those pictures in *Vogue* of high-bred Godivas riding by the sea with vacant expressions. One decides she is definitely out of her element here among the fluming pampas plumes. She extends a hand, speaking mechanically.

"Hello, how are you? I'm fine, thanks. Hello, so nice to meet you."

David indicates in sign language that this is the broker's daughter, then sweeps in behind her. "Didja meet Julia?"

"Julia who?" the girl whispers.

"Julia *you,* dummy. You want to give your real name?"

The wetsuit girl is angry. "David, you told me to be here at twelve, where's the *action?"*

"Justaminute, justaminute, I'm on the phone now." He starts toward the kitchen but the wetsuit girl stands fast at the front door, with her hand out. "I need cab fare," she insists. "Twenty dollars."

Under the bluewobbly light David rolls up two bills, presumably tens, and tucks them into the girl's wetsuit. This is another purpose of the dim lighting. "So she finds out in the cab it's two bucks," he explains. "Why should I give her twenty, because from twenty she'll want thirty, a week later she'll want forty."

"Don't you pay your girls?" says the director in middle-class shock.

"Pay is not a word. I take care of their clothes, doctor, dentist, hairdresser, their nightclub bills, liquor bills. But I pay for nothing! I get the clothes guy laid for nothing, the doctor, dentist, hairdresser laid for nothing, the limousine guy laid for nothing. Did you meet my John yet who owns all the garages, Leon? From Leon I get my limousines. See, I learned at a very early age what is the coin of this realm. *Women!* You can buy anything with beautiful women."

As if on cue, a woman named Darlene arrives at the door with three young maidens in modified Peck & Peck pants suits, whom she met at Maxwell's Plum. Darlene is the recruiter; David is the attraction. "I told them about this hilarious pimp I know," Darlene says.

"We just wanted to see," apologizes one of the curious girls. "I mean, we have to drive right back to Long Island—"

"Okay, into the bedroom and take off your clothes." David cuts straight through their timidity by parodying himself. Then jokes, flattery, a whirlwind tour of the penthouse, the *trompe l'oeil* bedroom, the vast round bed with an old Christmas tree beside it hung with three ornaments and varied lingerie—isn't it a riot, a Christmas clothes tree?—no one can be sure exactly *what* he said or if he was *really serious,* but wasn't he a riot? David gives them each his phone number.

Exit Maxwell's Plum recruits, consumed by the daredevil experience of meeting their first pimp. "And he's so sexy," whispers one to Darlene.

David makes a general announcement: one of these girls will call him within fifteen minutes. (Why string it out? A half hour later the phone rang. "Sweetheart!" David answered. "You sound like you're talking to me from inside a Campbell's Soup can—oh, from *Long Island.*")

Now, getting down to the business at hand.

"Now, Tom." David seats himself on the edge of a beanbag between the director and Julia, the broker's daughter. "What do you think? Isn't she a beautiful girl? And she's clean, no diseases, no colored men. She's a thoroughbred, you'd see her in Saks and she's another society girl, right?"

"She is a beautiful girl," Tom says, taking care to be no more than polite. His actress girl friend is observing closely.

"Only one thing. She hates men. Hates."

"Daayvid, I need a thousand dollars by the weekend." Julia pulls at his Levi's.

"Would you believe I broke this girl in at Saratoga racetrack? She tells the jockey, 'Don't kiss me, don't touch me, just get it over with.' The jockey says to me, 'I like this girl, she's a sexual freak.' "

"Daayvid, I have to go."

"She's a great hooker, Julia. Available any day from one to one ten. Busy, always busy."

Now Julia turns her frightened eyes, fully dilated, on David and his guests. A whisper: "The limousine company is calling and calling, I know they're going to do something terrible—"

"I told her to have the limousine company call *me*," David explains. "So I tell the limousine guy, 'Okay, I'll get you laid,' and I get him all hot for this great beauty who's available from one to one ten. She's not free!"

"Daayvid, please."

"Now, Tom, with your position, would there be amongst your friends a successful man who would take her on, a sugar daddy if you will?"

"I'd like that," Julia sighs, "somebody to take care of me."

At this point David's true artistry comes into play. By clowning, he blurs the line between natural pleasures and corruption.

"Okay, Julia, show us your breasts." Julia swallows her chin.

"One breast then."

"Oh, Daayvid," she whines, "the last time I did that nothing *happened*."

David bolts up and returns ruffling a copy of *Penthouse* magazine. "Keep your breasts—for ninety cents I can show Tom the best of the best."

"Daaaaayvid."

"Don't do this to me, Julia." David turns to the director with a tragic expression. "When she does this to me, I know she really needs the money. I mean, this is one girl I hated to corrupt."

"Oh, God, can't you help the poor girl?"

It's the actress. The bait has been nibbled and now the actress is prevailing on her boy friend to save the reluctant hooker with the heart of gold. The second-greatest pimp perks up. Time is fleeting. The big Johns are not calling. He will make do by hustling Tom for Julia, or the actress for Julia, or Julia and Tom while the actress watches, or the actress and Julia while Tom watches—this is classical pimposity!

"Okay," David suggests, "would you go with Tom for fifty dollars?"

"Fifty?" Julia shrinks.

"Look, you're a hundred-dollar chick but you gotta make adjustments in a recession, right? So you halve the price. Unless you'd rather go with Tom's girl friend. But you'd go with her free, right?"

"Well, ye-es."

The actress, embarrassed, says she'd like to use the ladies' room. Julia heads for the kitchen to phone her

163

child's governess. David follows both girls and, once free from scrutiny by the director, he suggests that the actress fondle Julia's breast. She does and smiles. "Tom, c'mon in here," calls the pimp. Tom comes around the corner leading with his ruffled shirt. "Look at Tom, what a classy guy. Isn't he beautiful?" Julia says he is very nice. "Go on, Tom, put your hand on her breasts." Tom obeys.

"Nice, isn't it?"

Tom says, "Marvelous." He keeps his hand on.

"All right, now you go," David encourages the actress. *Perfectly natural, everyone mauling the old mammaries for mutual pleasure, as it is written in the Kama Sutra.*

Tom says magnanimously to his girl friend, "Why don't you try it too?"

"I already did," the actress says.

"You *did!*"

A whole new region of jealousy splits the couple and a whole new territory is open for David. Divide and conquer. This is his normal modus vivendi, though on a much larger scale.

The telephone rings.

"Hello, Stanley the stockbroker!" David's eyes dance. "Yes and . . . yes and . . . we'll be right down."

He puts the actress on the phone. "Talk aquatic."

"Are you one of the swimmers?" the stockbroker asks the actress.

"I don't know exactly what I am right now," the actress says.

"Never mind, you just come down with David and we'll all have a beautiful swimming party."

The pimp kisses his dog good-bye. This is it. The beginnings of mathematical infinity. *Going for googol.*

1:30 A.M.

David opens the door of his cab for Valentino.

"This is one hooker I want you to meet, my Swedish beauty, one month in New York and she's already made $17,000." David quickly primes the actress, who has decided to accompany him "just to see."

From the shadows of an East Side club canopy the Fellini-esque figure materializes. A black sequin poncho glinting over her strawberry body stocking . . . a girlish face smiling, not a trace of guile . . . her eyes like Easter eggs, round, opaque, and colored-water blue—Valentino. She is licking a frozen custard.

David asks if she has cab fare.

"I have one dollar, yust now I am flat broke," the Swedish beauty says. Her complete equanimity suggests that the normal and healthy thing for one to do at 1:30 A.M. in Manhattan is to go to a pool party in a black sequin poncho.

The actress is fascinated. "Don't you, um, work?"

"It is not possible to work. In Paris, for exaaample," Valentino yawns over the long *a*, "we go out with men, all very close friends, and they yust put something in your purse. I mean it's so *normal* there's no discussing about it. A girl she cannot dress herself, look fantastic, stay up till four or five in the morning and, umm, offer herself with people which have a lot of money, and work too."

David takes credit for having weaned Valentino from scientology, which had become an expensive obsession. She is twenty-one and likes to travel.

"Mostly I am staying in the best hotels," Valentino adds. "I live very well. Yust now I am broke. I had a sum from my grandparents which I ran through. Here in New York I don't know anyone. David introduces me to gentlemen. But I am not desperate. As long as a girl is attractive—"

"Don't you find it *demeaning* to ask men for money?" the actress blurts, her cultural illusions showing like an American flag.

"What do you think most ladies have money from? From gentlemen." So perfectly natural, this Valentino. She never asks for anything, she simply has a good time and accepts the little gifts that go with it. And if she is lucky, as most of David's girls are, she will strike a John with a lonely fortune in sugar futures who will rush her into the connubial castle on the desperate illusion that she will repent, and all of this will come to pass before she is twenty-five and required to use her mind.

The cab slides across West 15th Street. Everyone steps out before a four-story brownstone and admires the stockbroker's neoteric renovation.

"Three dollars and fifty cents," the cabbie says. He is a young man with an *i* at the end of his name.

"What?" David explodes. "How'd you like to get laid for three fifty?"

The cabbie sniggers in disbelief. "I gotta take the car in to the old man now."

"Three dollars and fifty lousy cents to get laid by this beautiful Swedish scientologist!" David's voice climbs to a peak of incredulity. "All your life you'll beat yourself for passing this up."

Now the cabbie's mouth drops on the windowsill. "On the level?"

David beckons Valentino over and politely inquires if she would like to be cab fare. Valentino rolls her Easter egg eyes, no offense, no reaction—simply, no thanks.

"Okay," David turns back to the driver, "how'd you like to see a pair of boobs for fifty cents?"

The cabbie appears to be immobilized. Meanwhile, Valentino goes into the brownstone and comes down with four borrowed dollar bills and pays the cabbie, all in one movement as creamy as frozen custard filling up a cone.

Scents of clams and chlorine swim up behind Stanley the Stockbroker. He welcomes the guests into his pleasure palace. Not only does he have an Olympic-size pool, and two-story California cliffhanger windows affording a full view from the garden, and a sauna room, and cabanas, and a mezzanine deck outfitted with a long, professional clubhouse bar, but Stanley himself is a comely young bachelor. A mite paunchy, perhaps, but richly tanned and remarkably polite. He steps behind the bar to finish steaming his clams.

Why does a man like this need a pimp like David? The actress is mystified.

"Just watch," David whispers. "The guy with the smallest natural equipment is always the first one to say 'Let's get naked.'"

Within moments after David arrives, four girls of variegated dimensions and hair color are lined up at the stockbroker's bar, resembling an aberrant Miss Rheingold contest. David does not represent them as prostitutes. These are legitimate playgirls! David called them all for emergency fun—a mousy brown-haired anthropologist; an auburn-haired dropout from suburbia with large, insinuating hips; a spunky health instructor by the name of Luzanne; and Valentino, who falls passionately upon the clams.

One by one the young Johns file in. These are specimens from David's second string, owing to the short notice. (At this hour, his mature, six-figure patrons are asleep in the master wings of their suburban castles at a civilized remove from their wives.) One present John owns a chain of hosiery stores. Another belongs to the family that owns New York's favorite junk-food chain. And then there is Leon, the little caliph of Manhattan parking garages and the source of free limousines. They all look the same. Like men who spend too much time in 42nd Street movie balconies.

No one present seems to know the fundamentals of small talk. The girls say it's too cold to swim. The men attempt to describe their exploits at the track. Where's David? He is upstairs on the bed hearing confession from Luzanne, the health instructor. David: "So you went to St. Maarten with the congressman for three days, but did he comfort you with bread?" Luzanne is indignant. She would never take money, *directly*—she was quite content to islandhop in the congressman's chartered plane.

"That's right!" David roars with horselaughter, since this is the bill of goods he has been selling proud girls ever since Ellen the high school nymphet. "It is an art to be a high-class hooker. You can always say a man cannot buy you, because you do it for nothing!"

"Daaaayvid!" This time it is the anthropologist, calling from downstairs for social direction.

Now David the Pimp perches on the stairs above the bar, above them all. He beats the drums of the blood by telling what a great hustler he is.

"I go to the track day and night. But if my business is women, I'm supposed to take care of my women, spend time with them, the normal thing. I'm against that."

"You're against togetherness?" Luzanne pouts, tightening her grip on David's thigh.

"I'm against everything that's normal." He allows Luzanne his thigh. "So what happens is, I send my army of women out to the clubs. They pick up couples. They screen the men—like Manson's women, they know what I want. Now, every guy has one sharp girl, his best-looking girl. Upon getting the right freak, I am also getting a guy who has women. He's doing my work. In other words, the hours I'm at the racetrack, I'm in two places at once."

"But what can you do for a man who already has a sharp girl?" the actress asks. David's voice goes into fast-forward.

"I come home from the trotters, I park my limousine outside the club, my hookers bring out the Johns and their girls. Jingo—I blast them into a color TV, a beautiful bar, the whole thing. Now pretty soon I got *ten* guys and *ten* best-looking girls. Then I have a party for them. I'm very nice, a dullhead, I pass around the cocaine and pot—I let everybody go into the hustle. But all my hookers are there, you understand? Everybody's making a play for everybody else. Now, I induce two hookers to attack every guy. Then the best-looking girls who came up with these guys say, 'We're being made fools of.' Right! So I make a play for all of them. 'Girls, I'll meet you downstairs in my limousine, we're going to the Hippopotamus Club.' I knock out ten of them at once, why not? I've got an eight-door limousine. So while I'm getting ten guys laid from twenty hookers in my apartment, their girl friends go with me."

"That's genius," says the stockbroker.

"But how many of them will stay with you?" Luzanne evidently being new enough in the stable to have some dangling illusions about David's fidelity, sounds a singularly insolent note.

"Aha, that's only Part A of the genius," the pimp

continues. "Now what do I do with ten girls? I call up my good-looking Johns and my rich guys. But instead of giving them hookers, I give them straight girls. The girls don't know that these are Johns because *they're not hookers*. So the Johns pay me for girls who think it's a normal date!"

The garage owner downs his Scotch. "And all I can do is cheat at baccarat."

"Wait a minute." The twenty-four-hour worldbeater is not finished. "Then I go back to my apartment and tell the guys who I don't know in the first place that I need drastic money quick. Now who's gonna say no when he just got laid from two sharp hookers for nothing? So I get ten times my money there. I get ten times my money from the Johns at the Hippopotamus. Then I go to the track day and night, and that's how I live."

Applause all around.

Except for Luzanne. "Doesn't anybody ever get wise?"

"That's one of the things, see?" David leans down to his flock, who at this very hour are being manipulated in precisely the same fashion, and he croons into their deaf ears the basic principle upon which his attainments have been built. *"Nobody being hustled believes it."*

All heads nod, missing the point entirely.

"Let's everybody get naked!"

David winks at the actress. It is as he said. The first call comes from Stanley the Stockbroker, who is the first to strip and the first into the pool and who quite clearly possesses—among this bevy of strangers assembled by David the Pimp to fill the pool with aquatic delights—the smallest natural equipment.

That's it. That's the man's little weakness.

All join in the seraglio pool for preliminary water

games, followed by strip Chinese checkers, followed by sex, plain and fancy.

4:00 A.M.

"Who stole my dog?"

David thrashes about his apartment uprooting jungle plants and hurling beanbag cushions into the fluming pampas plumes. Valentino and Luzanne hang back, pulling fitfully on their wet hair. They have never seen David express emotion.

"I love that dog!" he shrieks. "Who stole my dog?"

The girls hear him opening the refrigerator door. Then a blunt sound. Over and over a blunt, tinny sound. It is David butting his head against a dog-food can. Then he disappears into the bathtub behind a black curtain and the girls, unequipped to handle the possibility that the second-greatest pimp might be weeping, go to bed.

At five the phone rings. No hand emerges from behind the black bath curtain. The phone rings confidently on for three dozen bells which means it could only be one person. Fannie White. Nice black telephone company lady who consults with businesses on the kind of service they require. She gave David his conference phone. She knows he is illegitimate, but she faithfully protects his lines. All David has to do is sing to her and make a little fun to her once a week. Nice lady.

"Fannie White? They stole my dog."

"Oh Davy, what'd you do?"

"I tried to feel it by banging on a dog-food can. Pimps can't feel, you know."

Fannie says she knows her Davy, he cries on the inside.

"I'm going to confide in you now, Fannie White.

There's only three things in this world I love. My dog, they stole that. My car, they're trying to repossess that. And——," leaving one blank, "I'm afraid the twenty-four-hour worldbeater is done. I can't hustle anymore."

Fannie White suggests he make a fresh start in the morning by phoning up his prosperous friends for help.

"I can't call any of my people, you understand? The image. I'm the laughing man, the big spender, they need me as their hope ship, I can't fail my people. Listen to me, Fannie White, my hooking business is down."

His phone bills look mighty healthy, Fannie says, why is his hooking business down?

"My prices are too high. Astronomical in fact."

The nice lady sings a few bars of the latest Blood, Sweat and Tears album. Nice. Indeed, David often borrows the name of David Clayton Thomas, his favorite singer, for meeting new people and signing bad checks.

"I can't sleep, Fannie White—too ashamed to call up my people for money—never worked in my whole life." David's voice dims out. When it returns, it carries the thud of doom.

"Do you think I should go to *work?*"

Oh, Jesus, Fannie White says, should the Lord sleep on Mondays? Before it comes to that, why doesn't David ask for help from his wife? (He has two bewitching former wives; but it is the second one, having gone on to richer glories, who is increasingly on his mind.)

"My wife is the third thing," says the pimp very quietly. "The other two things I love, my car and my dog, I love because her smell is on them." David slides deeper into his embryonic bathtub, letting his body dull and his feet float and the phone receiver bobble in the bath water until his inner ear is blocked.

"Beautiful girl, the most beautiful . . . didn't she double for Raquel Welch on location in Spain? . . . but who freed her from her uptight Anglo-Saxon bag? . . . I told her to take a hatchet to my car . . . oh, God, was that beautiful, my puritan wife in the country, high, laughing and axing the hell out of an eight-door limousine . . . but why couldn't she understand the hustler's weakness for people who are unhappy? . . . So a friend would call from Puerto Rico busted on a cocaine rap and I'd mail the rent money . . . how would I feel if a friend didn't come through for me? . . . I showed her the hustler's life but she only took one gamble, on one guy, on location in Spain . . . thanks for the telegram, baby . . . the score of scores and you made it . . . the fourteenth richest man in America . . . that's going for googol, baby."

DAVID CLAYTON THOMAS!

Fannie's voice burbles through his reverie. David steps out of the tub and turns his hair dryer on the phone receiver. "Sorry."

Fannie White says she is not feeling herself either. But she is scared to go out for her medicine on account of being alone.

"You called the right hustler!" David revives. "I'm on my way to the drugstore for you right now."

You'd do that for an old lady? The voice falters.

"What I wouldn't do—listen to me. My friend Carlo, the shylock, had a contracted killer out looking for him. Carlo was a vagabond. I took the guy in, co-signed a bank loan, took the responsibility with my number, my apartment. Last week Carlo split town and left me with his bill, $400. Now the shylock has *my* name. You don't know what hustling is like, Fannie White."

She says she'll go to sleep all right now, just knowing he'd go out for an old lady.

"About my wife," David picks up, "she just bought a $75,000 home in Westchester, just for the summer, y'know? For her boy friend. He's so rich his smallest company is one of the top three cosmetic firms. This guy makes $6,000 a minute!"

"Why don't you ask your wife for money?" the old lady suggests.

"It's all over. She's gay now. I send her girls. Then they come back and make love to me." David switches the hair dryer to HOT and turns it on his face. "That's how we keep in touch."

There is a knock on the bathroom door. Luzanne, sleep puffy, mumbles that someone is at the front door.

"Who, who?"

"Mmmmmm. Pino. G'nite."

"Is he a Puerto Rican guy with an orchid shirt?"

"Mmmmmm."

David says good-bye to Fannie White. He asks Luzanne to bring in his best suede suit. Four hundred dollars he does not have. Not even four. It will take some artistry to hustle one's own contracted killer out of killing one.

"Hello, Pino the Hit Man! How'd you like to take a bath with two beautiful hookers and I'll hold your gun."

It was a crime, David thought afterward, that neither Luzanne nor Valentino nor any of his people had seen him give one of the great hustles of his life. Looking his own murderer in the face, he had convinced Pino that his friendship was worth far more than four hundred dollars. Certainly more than a murder rap. In fact he talked him out of everything.

Pino decided it was much nicer to have a home

away from home. Hereafter Pino, too, will have unlimited visiting privileges in Penthouse H. That's it. That's the hooking business.

Now in the hot morning gloom, Luzanne slouches into the living room like an exasperated child. "Come to bed, David. Valentino tried to kiss me again. I can't sleep unless you're in the middle."

11:00 A.M. Friday.

Luzanne groans in her sleep. Someone is pressing against her, mauling, tickling. She gropes behind, along the outer circumference of the round bed, and comes into contact with a large mass of abdomen. Raising only the scrim of her lashes, she can see that David's body is in its natural place, running straight through the center of his bed like an arrow through a Valentine. On the other side of David is the sleeping Valentino. Luzanne puts her lips to the pimp's ear: "David, there are four people in this bed."

"Hi, I'm Baron bla bla," says a cheerful, heavily accented voice. "I was afraid you might go to the boat basin so I came early." A man's hand drops on Luzanne's shoulder. "Don't bother to get up."

Luzanne sits up and considers the middle-aged gentleman beside her. He is dressed as a boy, his top-heavy bulk encased in a blue denim shirt with a red hobo kerchief tied around his neck. His short, spindly legs are wedged close to hers. (His jeans are hung on the Christmas clothes tree with care.) Even before he stands, Luzanne can tell that the Baron's jeans will bunch up at the bottom.

"Where's your yacht?"

"My dear, I left Mamaroneck at six this morning to make a business breakfast with my directors at the Plaza at seven," the Baron explains.

"Some yacht party." Luzanne tugs at her halter top which is caught on a branch of the Christmas tree.

"I apologize." The Baron hands the health instructor her top, then motions toward a younger gentleman who has been standing, unacknowledged, in the doorway.

"Both Harvey and I have already put in five hours of work," the Baron announces. "Our time is limited."

"Very limited," says Harvey.

David unfurls from sleep like a paper party snapper, the tension of his ego so abruptly restored that it creates an explosion: "Let's have a round of applause for the Baron!" he bellows. "Some people don't understand the demands of high finance."

A great outboard motor of a laugh gurgles up from Baron bla bla. David enumerates the conglomerate owner's vast holdings (including a rich wife), and then gives a résumé of the Baron's friend Harvey. He owns a multimillion-dollar hotel management company. Meanwhile, unfazed, Valentino rises naked as the December snow and pads happily into the kitchen.

"Yust a minute for breakfast."

Luzanne, the perpetual pessimist, whispers something to David.

"Baron, c'mere," David says, "she wants to know why you get it off by giving me $1,000 for a girl."

In a sudden act of compulsiveness, the Baron pulls on his jeans and buckles up. He stands and clears his throat. "First of all, it's offered more *gracefully* here. One would never go to a madam and do this. Your first thought is you want legitimate girls. Contradict me if I'm wrong, Davy, you only know legitimate girls?"

"Of course!"

"And uhm," the Baron gazes fondly on the pimp, "Davy just has an amiable way of functioning. It's real-

ly as simple as that. He's laughs, fun, helps you over-
come your problems for a few hours in the afternoon.
It's better than going to a psychiatrist."

Valentino returns with a towel around her waist,
bearing a large glass plate which she extends to the
Baron.

"Would you care for some fried onions?"

He retreats, smiling limply, and stares in open-
mouthed wonder at the plenitude, the congeniality,
the right-out-*thereness* of Valentino's milkweed-pod
breasts.

"Will you look at the pair of eyes on this girl?" the
Baron exults.

David looks. "Valentino, will you go topless to the
races tonight?"

She acknowledges his question only with a small
upward roll of her eyes. Up, down, up, seeming never
to register or comment on anything that is said, it is
as though with each roll her Easter-egg eyes wash again
through the colored water and emerge depthless blue.

"No! She's a lady, why should she?" The Baron
answers for Valentino.

David looks from the rich little king to the penniless
playgirl, deciding how best to stimulate their self-de-
lusions and bring the two impostors together. "Let me
ask you something, Valentino, are you going to ball
him? Or would you like to do Luzanne, for money?"

The Baron picks up right on cue. "David, you're
very crude today."

"The way American men talk about sex, it lowers
your appetite." Valentino sits down to deliver her
soliloquy. Baron bla bla sits down beside her while she
eats her onion curds. She speaks into his wholly sympathetic eyes. "I find it disgusting, really, I mean what
do they think? That a girl likes to make love for noth-

ing? Even men of the overclass—"

"Upperclass," the compulsive Baron corrects, "but you're absolutely right."

"I mean it's not nice when a girl has to offer herself to go for money. She should yust be able to enjoy herself and go out with people and, umm, they yust give her a little present, no comment."

"Pre*cise*ly," says the Baron, "that's why I don't dig girls in the business."

The telephone rings. David picks it up in the bathroom; Luzanne follows and brushes his hair while he talks. Valentino returns to the kitchen to stir up another little mess. Harvey the friend remains straddled in the tiny hall between the bedroom, bathroom and kitchen, wiping his palms on his Meledandri bush jacket. The Baron sits alone on the far circumference of David's bed, listening to the pimp's laughter and song. *Hallelujah, you love me*—a broken Neapolitan tenor reverberates from the bathroom.

"Oh, God, I love this guy," the Baron murmurs. "He doesn't have a thing on his mind. How I'd love to be disorderly. You know me, Harvey"—he looks up at his friend—"I'm compulsively orderly and that's why I'm a success and that's why I'm miserable."

Valentino meanders back into the bedroom. "Dessert," she announces, spooning a wet mixture of condensed milk, sour cream, and lime into the Baron's mouth. "Who did you say you were?"

"Baron bla bla."

"Who is Baron bla bla?"

"I run bla bla corporation."

"Oh good! I have stock in that."

Valentino kicks the bedroom door closed with her bare foot.

Noon. David's girls begin to call.

JULIA *(the Wall Street broker's daughter):* I can't do it anymore.

DAVID: No more prostitution?

JULIA: I haven't been one, really.

DAVID: Oh no? Harold took movies of you screwing Leon in the car wash.

JULIA: Oh Daayvid, you're really awful.

DAVID: Awwww, I am not . . . shut up, SHUT UP! I want to show you something about me, Julia. I went there to Leon's car wash and they were showing the pictures in the back room. I burned the film.

JULIA: I really can't do it anymore.

DAVID: And I told Harold it was a very low thing he had done. Even in jest.

JULIA: You took care of it?

DAVID: Done.

JULIA: You get me very nervous when you talk about motion pictures. If my father—

DAVID: I scared you, didn't I? Now listen to me. *(His voice goes into high-speed double-talk.)* Your problems are my problems and I feel as graciously as possibly one can toward the nature of your problems that they can be undone one and all—you understand?

JULIA *(a whimper):* Oh, thank you, David.

DAVID *(exploding in half laughter, half sobs):* I love you, Julia, if it wasn't for you I'd never laugh, I love you, stupid.

JULIA: I still have the limousine company owner threatening me . . .

DAVID: Honey, all you gotta do is tell him David had four winners this week. You get him an interest, see? Horses. You tell him to call David.

The Baron steps out of the bedroom and announces he is leaving. Valentino ignores him and pads into the kitchen. David also ignores him, both hands occupied with arranging his hair before the bathroom mirror while he gives another virtuoso performance on the conference phone, which is tucked under his chin like a violin. The Baron moves toward the pimp's pocket.

"Don't/touch/that/pocket!"

David dances back like a matador. "You come to this apartment and you get something worth incomparable dollars for nothing. I have no price."

This seems to make perfect sense to the Baron. He collects his friend Harvey and trails into the hall encompassed in his own motorboat laugh, stopping only to assure the baffled Luzanne that David is an extraordinary person.

Luzanne slams the door. In a month of knowing David she has heard incessant gabble about vast sums of money, but she has never seen an actual dollar change hands.

"Didn't he offer you a thousand? How can you treat a Baron like that?"

The sound of her exasperation strikes a sensitive wound in the pimp. Why will straight women never understand that all of a hustler's money is *in transit* between his people, to be tapped and gambled on his way to the score of scores. This is the old hysterical sound of David's wife.

"It's only a game, understand?" The pimp catches Luzanne's flailing hands and spins her around and down like a tin top while he screeches out the instructions his wife never would understand. "I treat the sonofabitches rudely because they love it! Everybody else treats them with respect. They can't see in a million years what goes on here. I got Valentino to do the Baron compliments of New York City. A thousand dollars—that's not enough for a man worth millions. I do him a favor and he's never going to forget, understand? He's mine. That's the great art of my hustling!"

The girl spirals into a dizzy heap at David's feet. He bends down and pinches her mammaries.

"Ouch," she cries.

"That, my dear, is another word you'll have to forget if you're going to be a hooker."

1:00 P.M. More of David's people begin to arrive.

Elliot the Junketeer, a young man of weak but tanned good looks, enters wearing a new tiddlywinks tie. Elliot arranges junkets for businessmen on chartered flights to San Juan and Saint Maarten. A year ago David began to teach him that by including three or four hookers as a courtesy on these junkets, his business improves markedly. David rides along. He sets up a hospitality suite in the resort hotel to extend services through the junket. Many a pleasant four-day weekend is now passed in this way.

"Are you ready for a run to Saint Maarten, tomorrow?" Elliot asks, soberly businesslike.

"Ooh, can I go this time?" Luzanne is responding on schedule. There is nothing like a juicy island junket to add incentive to the recalcitrant call girl.

"Sure, but let me tell you about my junketeer." David faces Elliot as though his new partner is the villain of the piece. "I gotta let my hoors do him for nothing, and do the airline guys for nothing and the hotel managers for nothing and the croupiers for nothing and the pit bosses for nothing. They do so many guys for nothing to get on this junket, my hoors are too tired to make money from the customers. And this is the bastard who does it."

Elliot laughs off the charges. "These girls go for kicks. They don't care about supporting themselves. They manage from day to day, just like David. They live off people."

Luzanne takes to Elliot's sober style. Together they settle into a beanbag cushion and strike up an intimate acquaintance.

The next arrival is David's ex-orgiast. She is an investigator for clothing stores. Since retiring from partnership with the pimp, she provides an even more valuable service. She spies on his former wives. The last one developed some pretty kinky tastes.

David confronts the horsy woman at the door: "Did my second wife like the action I sent her last Saturday?"

"David you're caarazyee." The ex-orgiast chuckles.

"Speak!"

"She says she isn't taking anything from you."

His face slumps. "So next week I'll send her something a little more exotic." No time for depression. On the heels of his ex-orgiast, David's crooked horse trainer arrives. Terry works out the horses in the morning and bloats the favorite with water so that by afternoon he can tell David which horse will not win.

And then Julia arrives. The broker's daughter, having only an hour before renounced this life of sin, is dressed and ready for the races in the latest drop dead patchwork suede number from Stephen Burrows' collection at Bendel's. But weeping.

"Daaayvid, I need $200 by tomorrow."

"The limousine company?"

"No, no, I took care of them. It's this emerald watch I charged. The jeweler keeps calling and I know he's going to do something terrible—"

David folds the fallen sparrow under his wing and turns to his people, transported to a region of delight known only to jugglers of the flesh. "I love my girls. Look at this mess I'm in now, I can't even buy them coffee. Still they come back to me."

Everyone gathers round the pimp's glow to see what will happen next. He looks at Julia's emerald watch.

"Three thirty! We'll arrive just in time for the ninth race. That's class."

At Belmont Park David marches his exotic retinue directly up to the top terrace, the private Turf and Field Club. Everyone seems to know him. He frisks about introducing his new girls to the horseplayers. Now he studies the boxes. Moments before the ninth race a gentleman owner leaves his box. David stiffens like a pointer.

"That's the sign. Sole Mio will win."

He collects a total of $1,600 from his flock and bets only to win. Sole Mio places fifth. But wait—here comes Terry the crooked horse trainer, waving a fistful of his own mutuel tickets.

"A winner, he's gotta winner!" David dances to the window behind Terry. "We go to the trotters tonight."

Coming out of Belmont Park surrounded by his junketeer, his ex-orgiast, his Swedish scientologist, his health instructor, his beautiful broker's daughter, his crooked horse trainer, and a gaggle of jockeys, David is again a happy man. Seventy cents in his pocket. But all of his people are sticking with him. "That's the hustler's life," he says, piling them into his eight-door limousine.

On the expressway his eye is caught by another limousine, chauffeur-driven, with a middle-aged man huddled in back all alone against the gray felt. The pimp swerves across his lane.

"Does he need a friend?" David shouts at the chauffeur.

The chauffeur grins. His lips move and the man in back smiles and the chauffeur rolls down his window. "What have you got?"

"What have I got!"

At seventy miles an hour David the pimp squeezes his chariot into an intimate embrace with the other limousine. He extends a hand-lettered card, bearing an address in the East 70s, through the window to the driver.

"I got a party going tonight for the richest men in America *and* their chauffeurs. Penthouse H—H for hooker."

Veering off, David pumps the accelerator and jolts ahead. Seventy-five, eighty, eighty-five, his mind races the little white needle as he plots the evening ahead—he will put the limousine owner and the crooked horse trainer together with the broker's daughter and the health instructor and have the chauffeur drive them to the Hippopotamus where his regular hookers will be waiting with new Johns to break up the couples, while he himself repairs to Leon the garage owner's $100 table at Yonkers Raceway with his junketeer and his ex-orgiast and his Swedish scientologist to recruit new faces for Saint Maarten and then everybody will come back to Penthouse H and from there who knows? That's it. That's going for googol.

The clock outside the Midtown Tunnel reads 5:00 P.M. The beginning of a whole new twenty-four hours. David glides through the exact-change lane without stopping.

Chapter Seven

"Working for a pimp is lousy." said the married
call girl in apartment 7-V, "Work for a house,
and the madam's working for *you*."

"We Yorkville madams run a clean business,"
insisted the housemother beside her in 7-V.

"I'm a prisoner in a $500 apartment
in the biggest red light district in New York!"
wailed the Junior League mother in 7-U.
"Can't *somebody* help me get rid of . . .

"THAT MADAM NEXT DOOR"

The very first conference between feminists and prostitutes in Manhattan degenerated into a brawl. The
two-day meeting in January 1972 was run by middle-
class panelists in combat boots who wanted to save
their sisters of the musk-oiled flesh. Surprise: a few
white-collar call girls turned up to speak for themselves. They were not only articulate but also in total
disagreement with their would-be saviors, whereupon
the liberated panelists brushed them off as uppity. The
feminists were determined to come up with a clear-cut
position on the issue.

FEMINIST: It's the most degrading thing a woman can
    do.
CALL GIRL: Bullshit.

FEMINIST: We all have to make sacrifices if we want to be free.

CALL GIRL: You have to realize you're frightened of us. Because it's your husband's, your bosses, your radical-hip boy friends who come to us.

FEMINIST: It's not like we are Movement women who are all theory . . .

At this point women in the audience began compulsively to confess their own degradations, *actual experiences* with whoring, so the prostitutes would understand they were only trying to help. "It's hard for me to talk . . ." faltered Susan Brownmiller, an otherwise fearless feminist, but fifteen years ago as an ambitious waitress she had turned a few tricks. "I was a very bad prostitute. It was the most horrible experience of my life," she said.

FIRST CALL GIRL: Bullshit!!

SECOND CALL GIRL: I'm really tired of all of you talking about the *degraded* prostitute. You cannot sit here and make decrees about 50,000 to 75,000 prostituting women. At least get to know the different types. For instance, the streetwalker is becoming obsolete. She's been replaced by massage parlors and high-priced call girls. A whole new working breed is coming out of the ranks of office workers and secretaries.

Of course, the naked eye tells any New Yorker that street hustlers are far from obsolete. That wasn't the point. The call girls were simply exhibiting the fierce class snobbery that exists within the hierarchy of their profession. In fact, no one is more offended by the bad reputation growing up around a new breed of violent street prostitutes than their more elevated sisters within the calling.

Most call girls have solidly middle-class aspirations: home, husband, family, comforts. But first they want to climb to the highest cash position they can reach and cast their nets from there. Since their occupation is at least temporarily illicit and illegal, they exhibit a strong need to legitimatize themselves in the eyes of "normal" people—especially straight women. Here they were, then, a row of prostitutes who had come out at the highly unprofessional hour of 9:00 A.M. for this diddlepoop conference, and by now they were hopping mad.

CALL GIRL: So fuck off, feminists, and don't call us, we'll call you.

Feminists began to leave, crying, shattered. Several feminists fell upon a woman reporter—"Let's beat her up"—and to show their fearless loyalty, they grabbed the tape from the woman's tape recorder and turned it over to a prostitute.

Unimpressed, the call girl seethed: "I exposed my tender ass to come here today." A radical feminist observed that her sisters took a risk starting the whole women's movement three years ago. *Swock!* Prostitute slugged feminist. *Drubble.* Feminist broke into sobs. The conference went to pieces on the spot.

Working girls see feminists in very basic, competitive, American capitalist terms. "They're trying to butt into everything, grab the publicity and wreck our business. How many of them can make $1,000 a week lying down?" a call girl I later met summed up the prevailing attitude.

I too have sympathy for prostitutes. Especially for the unfairness of exacting all penalties for our moral hypocrisy from working girls, while the police run them through our revolving doors of justice, the pimps and Johns go free, and the moguls of the organized porno-sex industry keep right on raking in the money from their massage parlors, prostitution hotels, peep shows, luxury apartment houses and what have you. But it does seem a waste of effort, at this point, for the women's movement to dwell on the "correct" ideological position to take on prostitution. There are so many other women out there—waitresses, secretaries, steelworkers' wives, the middle-aged and the unmarriageable—all hovering on a raised consciousness and needing only a helping hand to pull them over the line. It stands to reason that only as these more motivated women open up new options and alternative life patterns will the intransigent prostitute feel an inclination to follow. But the first duty of redeemers is to educate *themselves*. If you want to alienate a prostitute with your first pitch, offer her blind sympathy.

Indoor prostitutes maintain they are the only honest women. The exchange of flesh for money is transacted in a businesslike way, concluded within the hour, no adolescent notions or romantic emotions about it. How many of us have taken the trouble to find out what the call girl's work has to offer *her*?

Many working girls, when they are new in the city, spend at least a few months with a madam in order to meet the better Johns. A cheap house offers girls for a dollar a minute. "She just lets the guy in, washes him off, milks him and throws him out," says a veteran. But the nice houses in Yorkville are far more accommodating, and expensive. Here the enterprising madams take a 40 percent cut if the girl lives out, a 50 percent to 75 percent share if she lives in. The cut is for linen, liquor, protection and introduction to the John, all of which the madam provides. The only thing she withholds at all costs is the phone numbers of her clients.

Now, what the working girl has in mind while doing her stint with a madam is to build up her own "John Book." Madame Xaviera Hollander, for instance— who at the age of twenty-eight claimed before the Knapp Commission to Investigate Alleged Police Corruption that she was the proprietor of New York's highest-class flesh palace—purchased a John Book from her predecessor for 10,000. Most girls don't want to pay. So they remember where the John works and call him later at his Wall Street office: "Remember me? I met you at Madame Lazanga's. . . . Well, I have my own apartment now."

Not all girls care to move out of the madam's cushy setup to climb the professional ladder on their own. For the swelling ranks of suburban housewives who prefer part-time work turning tricks, rather than running bedpans around the local hospital, the convenience of a madam in Manhattan is perfect. But for the ambitious young career woman, nothing will do until she becomes an independent.

By the strangest coincidence, I received my early education in caste and class within the hustling trade all in one building on the upper East Side of Manhattan. Clermont Towers is a luxury high-rise on the corner of 82nd Street and York Avenue. It's an innocent-sounding address, but then all the best brothels are in Yorkville. My education began with a call to *New York* magazine from one of the straightest ladies in Manhattan, a Mrs. Hogan. By chance I took the call.

Mrs. Hogan was distraught. She had been on the

phone all morning, repeating her story and pleading for help: "That woman next door threatened to kill me! I'm alone with three young children. My husband's in Brazil. My baby-sitter's gone for the weekend and I'm afraid to go out." She had called her local precinct, her congressman, her rental agent at Amprop, her doctor, her lawyer, all her friends in the Junior League and her husband's colleagues on Wall Street. She had reported her plight to the Third Division's "pross squad" and the Police Department Community Relations Division and, God save her, she had even called the Knapp Commission. At noon she dialed *New York* magazine. By now Mrs. Hogan was hysterical.

"I'm a prisoner in a $500 apartment in the biggest red-light district in New York! Can't somebody help me?"

It seems that six months before, Mrs. Hogan's expanded family had moved into apartment 7-U in Clermont Towers and "that woman" had moved into 7-V. "That woman" was an alleged madam operating an alleged brothel right next door to Mrs. Hogan, which in itself was putting this Catholic mother through a little bit of purgatory every day. Her children, coming home from the Dalton School, were required to pass daily through a lineup of the madam's clientele. "These unsavory characters pat my children on the head and make remarks—'Hello, sonny'—you know, nothing dangerous, but the whole idea is so—*tawdry*."

Mrs. Hogan had never actually seen the alleged madam, but she had a particularly vivid concept of what was going on next door. A graduate of Sacred Heart Academy, Mrs. Hogan had already accumulated nine years on the benches of Carl Schurz Park cataloguing, along with other Junior League mothers, what seemed like the inexorable moral decline of Manhattan. And now, of course, every night was proving her correct. Together with Mr. Hogan, a Wall Street attorney, she was forced to endure the din of degenerate parties and lewd conversations which passed clearly into their bedroom through what the rental agent alleged to be a wall. The Hogans had not slept soundly for six months.

This morning the matter had come to a life-and-death confrontation. Mr. Hogan had been away all week on business. Mrs. Hogan reported: "I came home from driving him to the airport and my baby-sitter said, 'Ugh, it's been just awful.' You see, I'm locked in here at night, I hear a lot of the noise my neighbors don't hear. Well, at six o'clock this morning they were at it in there again, fighting over money, you know, and I got up and went out into the hall for the milk and newspaper. I tried to call the desk downstairs to complain but nobody answered so I lost my cool. I pounded on her door and said, 'Shut up!' With that the police came down the hall.

"I said to them, 'Well, thank goodness, somebody else called the police and I'm not alone around here. With that woman next door you can't sleep in this place!' I closed my door and my son Tommy gets up. He's five. Well, I was in the bathroom when the phone rang and Tommy answered and it was *that woman*. God knows what she said to him but he reacted by getting overstimulated. He began singing and dancing all around the living room and carrying on wild, I mean *hysterical*. The phone was ringing again. I just picked it up and waited because I knew exactly who it was going to be. And she said to me, *'You're dead now.'*"

Mrs. Hogan paused for breath while her sorry tale

was passed around the *New York* office. Occasionally she would groan, "Can't somebody down there help me?" At the time I was engaged in research on several street-prostitution stories, but I had never met a madam in my life. Notwithstanding, I was dispatched as a sort of vigilante baby-sitter for the beleaguered Hogan family.

On the subway, quite frankly, I could not keep my mind entirely on poor Mrs. Hogan. Visions of the great bawds and legendary brothels of New York and those Chinese bagnios on the old Chicago Levee danced through my imagination. Would "that woman" next door be like Polly Adler? My sources had spoken wistfully of the many evenings they climbed those hallowed stairs on Sixth Avenue and 55th Street for a midnight omelet at Polly's club. Polly kept an accomplished chef and the drinks were a dollar apiece and the gossip ran like bathtub gin alternating with the champagne of cultured discourse. Such ambience!

Perhaps "that woman's" brothel in Clermont Towers, catering to upper East Side swells and all, would be more refined—along the lines of the Everleigh Club. Seldom in the lore of whoredom has anyone assembled so many sensual luxuries for so discriminating a clientele as did Ada and Minna Everleigh in their fifty-room mansion on Chicago's Levee. They put $200,000 into the furnishings alone. Splendidly jeweled and observing perfect etiquette, the Everleigh sisters would lead gentlemen in dinner clothes up the mahogany staircase to their choice of public rooms. They might dine with gold cutlery on the rare patina of a fifty-seat refectory table. Or languish on slippery damask divans, listening to hand-picked ladies play the golf-leaf piano. And then on to the private parlors, a décor for every whim—Moorish, Turkish, Japanese, Egyptian, one with walls of hammered copper—each an all-consuming womb of silken bolsters, a rhapsody of fountains splurging perfume.

Such are the madams of which great cities can boast.

Right up front, Mrs. Hogan's building did not strike me with its ambience. Clermont Towers looked like a very large cardboard egg container: spongy grayed brick façade, two wings symmetrically scored and evenly pocketed with windows, similar in all respects to the other great egg boxes of Yorkville. At the height of the recession in the fall of 1970, the renting business was so slow that agents would shove anybody into these buildings: one month's deposit, no references, no lease, stay as long as you can. For madams, pimps, prostitutes, pushers, heads, freaks, orgiasts, ax murderers and all manner of petty crooks, it was heaven. For your ordinary, dull, paying tenant, complaints brought worse than no results. In a typical in-out-nobody-gives-a-damn building at 233 East 69th Street, where rents go beyond $550 a month, police records showed over forty arrests on prostitution charges in the year ending April 1971. It was particularly unhealthy to be suspected by an arrested tenant of having been the complaining tenant. The lawyer husband of a Junior League officer carped one evening, in his elevator at 505 East 79th Street, about a neighboring madam. She happened to be in the elevator too. Before they stepped out she lunged at the lawyer with a knife and left a seventy-two-stitch gash across his face. He did not press charges.

Mrs. Hogan's Valium arrived at the same time I did.

Mrs. Hogan was a lean, erect matron with a pony tail and black patent Guccis. Greeting me in a subdued funk, she poured us each a double Scotch. "Did you see anything coming in?"

I had to say I had seen nothing.

"But you noticed the sign on her door? *Venire.* It's the Latin word for *to come.* Disgusting."

Had her landlord responded at least? Had the police come?

"The building manager said if I make any more trouble they'll evict *me,* no matter if my best friend is John Lindsay," Mrs. Hogan said. "The police I threw out. They said if this had happened anywhere else in the country they'd have the authority to go in and *boom boom,* that would be it. But this city has hit its lowest ebb. They said I should write letters to the D.A. and the mayor because their hands are tied."

Mrs. Hogan's son, Tommy, began to laugh, which set her three-year-old daughter to crying. "Don't you care?" she wailed. "Mommy might get dead!"

Surely that woman next door must have been arrested before?

Well, yes, Mrs. Hogan knew of three raids. But each time the woman was back the same night. The third time a city marshal came and dragged all the madam's furniture into the hall; the Hogans went on a vacation to celebrate. But on their return all was as before—bankers in low-profile hats prowling the hall and the Latin types and the Japanese Johns bowing and scraping. "She has an international clientele. And now she's more blatant than ever," Mrs. Hogan adds. "Since she beat her eviction, she doesn't give a damn. She knows she can get a $500 apartment almost anywhere on the upper East Side."

For owners and operators who manage many buildings in New York City, and whose rental agents masquerade under dozens of different names, the situation is golden with profit. When a tenant wants to complain, there's no one to call because the managing agent is a name behind a nameplate inscrutably linked to a string of shell corporations. Mrs. Hogan never did get anywhere with her managing agent, which went by the name of Amprop.

She had already made up her mind to move to Florida. It is always going to be cleaner, safer, sounder, more honest, upright and moral somewhere else. Miami, Minneapolis, Detroit, Boston, Oakland, Chicago —anywhere but that well-known citadel of vice and crime, New York. The *facts* are: New York receives the majority of its street prostitutes from Minneapolis, Detroit, and Boston. Oakland and Chicago both have 25 percent more murders than New York (24 homicides per 1,000 population). And Miami has exactly *twice* as many murders as our misunderstood town. I tried to tell Mrs. Hogan about Miami—but she wasn't remotely interested.

"Just tell me, what is that sickly sweet smell?" she asked, leading me into her bedroom to press a nose against the wall.

"Smells like someone is cooking pot stew," I said.

"That's it! That's how she gets people from the building on her payroll, she feeds them. The desk man told me she sends down leftovers from her parties."

On Mrs. Hogan's night table was a bottle of Lysol and an inspirational library including Bishop Fulton Sheen, Kahlil Gibran, St. Theresa of Avila and *No Bars to Manhood* by Daniel Berrigan. As she talked on about the corrupt police and morally bankrupt mayor and the liberals, intellectuals and the kids, how she distrusts them all—"feeding the Communists, taking over, everyone being on the devil's payroll these days" —I began to wonder about Mrs. Hogan. One could imagine her lying in bed, driven by fantasies of those foul bodies next door, sending off spirochetes of moral disease which actually seemed to *seep* through her walls.

At that point Patrolmen McKeever and Speer arrived. "Did you see anything coming in?" Mrs. Hogan whispered. *"That woman next door?"* The police said no, but they'd knock and find out. At last the door to 7-V opened. A pleasantly plump woman in pink Capri pants welcomed them in. "I just put on some fresh coffee," she said.

"Name," said the cops.

"Venire."

"Did you call and threaten the lady next door?"

"Never! She's driving me crazy," the woman in Capri pants exploded. "Noise, noise, she lets her kids run wild up and down the hall all night, I can't sleep! Some people would keep their little brats inside. Not her, she's after me. *I* called the cops on *her*."

Patrolmen McKeever and Speer came back rubbing their chins. "Well, what happened, what was she like?" demanded the triumphant Mrs. Hogan.

"Like you, lady, just like you."

Having kept the vigil until evening, I was relieved when Mrs. Hogan's robust colleague from the Junior League arrived with her weekender case. I passed 7-V more slowly on my way out, my ears straining for evidence of lascivious pursuits. The only sounds were ticking and laughter. *Did she time her clients?* Pressing closer to the door—oh dear, this was very embarrassing. I had obviously fallen prey to Mrs. Hogan's shut-in paranoia. The woman next door was watching "Beat the Clock."

A week later, while waiting around the Manhattan Criminal Courts Building, I was invited to join the prenoon club of prostitution lawyers for "a few belts" at Happy's Bar. A hardy half-dozen of these pross lawyers handle almost all the regular working girls. The lawyers all grew up on the Bronx streets and have found happiness in Long Island with maids and swimming pools. As the lunch crowd drifted away, the hard-core fraternity was left: lawyers, bondsmen, and cops who live off the "legal" proceeds of prostitution. A man I'll call "Cisco," the shortest and most timid of these pross lawyers, asked if I would like to meet a madam. "I done her a lot of favors when she was just turning tricks," he said. "Now she's a big-time brothel matron." I was more than delighted with the idea.

Driving uptown, Cisco the Lawyer told about the latest thing in prostitution—swing parties. "For $200 you get a whole night of group sex. The TV personalities and their wives love it. But me, I like my privacy."

My mind was on the neighborhood we were entering, Yorkville. My imagination raced ahead to those legendary brothels with the Cordon Bleu chefs and gold pianos. Cisco parked. "Here we are."

"But this is Clermont Towers."

"That's right, the madam's been in here for six months."

"Seventh floor?"

"Seven-V, right."

"And the sign says *Venire*, right?" To display my familiarity with the lower depths, I add, "That's Latin for *to come*."

"Venire's her *name*, honey." The lawyer's eyes

abruptly narrow. "How do you know Carol Venire?"

"Oh I don't, I don't, but you know"—casting about to cover myself—"happy people talk and great reputations spread."

"Carol, it's Cisco," the lawyer calls through the door of 7-V. "I brought a friend wants to see how you do business."

"She's not one of those greasy women's lib types, is she, 'cause if I ever get my hands on—"

"No, no, she's just a regular broad that wants to educate herself."

Still bargaining through her peephole, Carol Venire says she will have us in to play some cards and eat supper. "Tonight will be dead anyway because the goddam phone is out of order. But no questions about my business," she warns. "We're very sensitive in this profession, you know."

Thus did Madame Venire finally open the door for a full view of her flesh palace.

Everything is covered in plastic. The place is furnished in Italian Time-Payment Provincial. A sign on the Formica bar specifies: DONATION, $1. Beyond it, lying face down under a coat on the convertible sofa, is a young woman, snoring.

"You people ravenous, I hope?" Carol Venire says. "I have veal scallopine on the stove and Spanish rice. Nobody appreciates my cooking around here—in, out, everybody's always running in and out." She runs a weary hand through her frosted hair and across her plucked black brows. She is again wearing pink Capri pants and an aqua halter. The face, rather ordinary, fortyish and without makeup, suddenly lights up in a cap-toothed smile. "You play blackjack?" She pulls a roll of $20 bills out of her waistband.

"Not awfully well," I falter. "And I haven't more than $20 with me."

"That's okay, honey," clucks the madam, looking me over, "we can always take your losses out in trade."

Terrific.

I am relieved when Madame Venire remembers her vocation and rushes to the kitchen phone. "Whaddya mean you can't send a man up here to fix my phone before tomorrow! I run a *service business.*"

I walk into one of the bedrooms to plan my strategy. The four-poster bed is layered with hotel-supply sheets and towels. A stuffed lion sits on the headboard. I have never seen such a collection of disinfectants, vaginal sprays, gargles, and surgical cleansing soaps as are displayed in Madame Venire's bathroom. At that point Cisco the Lawyer reels into the bedroom, having smoked a joint on top of his afternoon tankard of gin. He falls across the four-poster. Since the phone is out of order and the lawyer is now unconscious and the only friend within thirty blocks' reach is Mrs. Hogan, I decide to be scrupulously nice.

"Let's get some music in here, this place is dead," Madame Venire was saying as I came out. She flips *Sombra, the Spider Woman* off the telly and shoves a cartridge of Jackie Gleason into the stereo. Then she beckons me into the dining room where two boys in satin shirts are slumped over a spotless glass table. "Who's gonna deal?" No response. She brings out a bottle of Windex and rubs the glass table to a veritable mirror.

"Wake up and drink," she orders, setting out coffee cups. "Mama wants to play on her night off."

The Long Island boy reaches for a Diet Mazola container filled with pot. Without looking, he rolls himself a joint. Brightening, he nudges the boy next to him.

"Hey, Ralphie, look alive." Ralphie continues to look dangerously pale and seems to have no other function in life beyond being a dropout from the University of Bridgeport.

At the sound of shuffling cards the sleeping girl on the sofa stirs. The two boys go over and blow smoke in her face. She rises and comes to the glass table with a blanket over her head. "Hit me." Between hands she puts her head on the table and naps.

"This is Didi, Ralphie, the Kid, and what's your name? Gail," Madame Venire does the introductions in the manner of a mother hen. "Okay, it's a buck a point. Hit me, kid. I'll stay. Wheeee—pay twenty-one!"

I had some trouble keeping my mind on the game. Every half hour the madam would order, "Okay, everything off the table," and come round with her Windex bottle to scour the glass in front of us. Then she would ask the time and rush in to check her scallopine pots. "Both my wrist watches are broken," she complained, tugging at the diamond-jeweled pocket watch hung around her neck on a pajama string. "I stole it off a customer." She giggled.

Every so often Ralphie the Dropout would focus and recite from the *Bhagavad Gita*. But there was absolutely no asking the madam about the brothel business. My questions elicited nothing but more hostility.

"Most of you straight women are filthy. You don't know how to take care of your bodies. *You're* the whores. I run a class house." She looks around the table for affidavits. "Ask Didi here. I can't tell you how many out-of-town businessmen have come up here and thanked God they found me after two or three bad experiences with straight girls."

"Yeah," mumbles Didi, wrapped in her own arms.

"Working for a pimp is lousy. You work for a house and the madam's working for *you*." Now Didi looks up for the first time, probably supposing I am a new recruit. She is a busty little thing about twenty-five with lustrous black hair to her waist and a large set of engagement and wedding rings.

"You're not married, are you?" I ask.

" 'Course. You don't think I do this all the time. That's no way to live." Didi tosses me a locket with her little boy's picture inside. "I have a beautiful home in Long Island. My husband's just starting his own talent agency, booking belly dancers and all that, a very lucrative business. If he had his way I wouldn't be working. It's me, I want to make enough to really invest in this business and then retire."

Didi asks Madame Venire for some Sara Lee pound cake.

"Dinner's coming. You gotta watch your weight." The madam pats the call girl's meaty arm and smiles approvingly. "My girls come to me, I check them out," she says. "We Yorkville matrons have a clique, you might say. We always call each other for references on new Johns and working girls. 'Course they'll steal a good trick as soon as look at you, but the protection is still worth it. Otherwise you never know when you'll get a freak or a cop or a street girl with a dose."

Didi says she has the perfect setup here. She leaves her family out in the country with a housekeeper and comes into the city to stay with Madame Venire for two or three weeks at a time. "I make my money and go back home to rest for maybe a month."

Such distinctions are terribly important to prostitutes on their way up. The streetwalker/$25 hooker/whore-addict belongs in the blue-collar end of the business. Any girl operating in one of the white-collar slots as a self-respecting call girl, like Didi and those at the feminist conference, voices contempt for the street hooker. Madams look down their noses too, and Venire was no exception: "A street girl turns vicious in three weeks," she explains after I do some prodding. "None of the matrons will touch them. Besides, they have no respect for us, they call us *flatbackers*." Her nostrils flare; the contempt is mutual on the part of both classes of prostitutes. But there is more to it—there is pure financial competition and a great deal of jealousy. I ask Madame Venire about this.

"Didn't I tell you no questions about my business?"

Just this one, I coax. "Is it true that street girls generally gross more money than call girls? Say $70,000 a year, as compared to the average $50,000 a full-time flatbacker in a house such as yours can expect as annual gross income?"

"Street girls can use knives, roll a guy for $1,000. So of course they can make more money than us." The madam's tone of voice is indignantly self-righteous: once again, virtue is *not* its own reward. "We madams are up here in our houses like sitting ducks. We run a clean business. We gotta, the cops have our phone numbers!"

I sympathized.

"C'mon, c'mon, we've only got time for a few more hands before dinner," the madam snaps. "When I was a dealer in Vegas I used to make $700 in a couple of hours." She shuffles through the heap of twenties beside her cards. "Mmmmm, push."

Suddenly I am down $19 with a dollar left. Suppose this is how she traps all her white slaves?

"Well?"

"Hit me," I say, a true bluff artist.

"Pay the dealer."

Thank God for the housemotherly blood in Madame Venire. Just as I reach financial ruin, her oven timer goes off.

"Okay! Everything off the table," she orders. "I can't stand to serve on a dirty table."

Madame Venire is back with her Windex bottle. I fumble with my cards, cigarettes, the cat in my lap—what to do with the damn coffee cup? I slide it onto the laminated plastic chair beside me.

An ominous pause.

"Who set that coffee cup on my chair?"

Everyone looks innocently back at the madam. She zeroes in on me, her face suddenly bleached with rage.

"What do you think I am, an animal!"

"But it's covered with plastic," I stammer, motioning helplessly toward the chair.

"You straight women are all alike. No manners, no respect. I don't allow *pigs* at my table. You treat this house as if it were your home—"

I go in and sprinkle cold water on Cisco the Lawyer. "I think she wants us to leave."

What has the urban style come to, I am thinking, when even the brothel, that proverbial palace of nectareous delights, is crammed into a sterile modern apartment . . . when the perfumed fountains and silken hassocks give way to laminated plastic and Formica . . . when the Cordon Bleu chef is replaced by Sara Lee . . . and when in place of great bawds with the wit, wile and impeccable etiquette of an Adler or Everleigh, we have a disinfectant freak in Capri pants who operates like the matron of the Biltmore restroom? Oh, well, what with high rents, poor city services and the servant problem, I suppose the brothel is just another casualty of creeping mediocrity.

I go back to say good-bye to the card game. Madame Venire, only midway through her stream of invective, draws a deep, infuriated breath.

"—I'm a sensitive woman. But you, if I was as pushy as *you*, I'd be a wealthy woman today. You're all alike, you and that crazy lady next door!"

That was my exit cue.

A few months later I heard that Madame Venire had moved to another Yorkville high-rise to take the heat off. But by then the Hogan family had already fled to Miami . . . only to find that their new building was managed by the same outfit. So it goes.

Chapter Eight

Respectability begins when a girl needs
nothing but her wits, a good wardrobe and
her telephone to work. Graduated beyond
pimps and madams, bearing her old scars
silently, she likes to think of herself as . . .

THE LIBERATED
CALL GIRL

"Take a woman of my age. Twenty-five. Divorced. After a woman has lived with a man and reaches a certain age, she needs sex. That's why being a working girl to me is so great. When I'm horny I can come with my clients. I take only champagne tricks, $100 an hour. My men are all very well-dressed and successful with styled hair and young wives in Southampton, that group. They're men I would date if I weren't in the business. It's a protection for me because I'm always afraid of getting involved. I don't want another unhappy marriage. So being a call girl is like taking out sexual insurance. I get paid for it. Plus when I want to enjoy it, I enjoy it."

I am sitting in the apartment of an independent call girl on Central Park South four days before Christmas. In prostitution circles, Christmas is known as the slowest season of the year. Other people's husbands are busy erasing the resentment in their children's eyes with a few days of family togetherness. After Christmas they take their wives to the Bahamas, returning only to face the swollen charge accounts of February. For the young woman sitting across from me, the next month always takes the shape of an egg, a sucked-out egg—barren, weightless, cornerless, qualified only to roll and roll . . .

The woman looks disturbingly like me. Since she won't be working tonight, she has chosen her own favorite sleeping costume: a football jersey. Her skin is spotted with medicated cream. From one cigarette she lights another; she is anxious to please. Yet her deathly pale face remains immobile as a dinner plate. The only moving, uncontrolled parts are the corners of her mouth. As she talks numbly about her past and catalogues the acts of self-annihilation that she invites four and five times every night, the corners of her mouth tremble as though at any moment she might cry. But if she once began, she would never stop.

*

"I've had every experience a girl could have and every one of them has been a humdinger. I got pregnant the day before I went to boarding school. We made love out in the fields. My boy friend and I, in Baltimore, before my parents sent me away. I found out two months later. What could I do about it in an uptight private school in upstate New York? I had no money. So I ran away to New York and did some modeling for a nudie magazine. I didn't let on I was sixteen until they paid me. That way, they couldn't use the pictures but I got the $150 anyway.

"Someone gave me the name of an abortionist in West Harlem. But what happened was, I was walking on Ninety-second Street in broad daylight and this black guy hit me over the head. I remember his eyes when I woke up, they were like a lizard's. He was holding me and rocking me and saying 'Stop screaming at me!' I wasn't screaming at all. There was a knife pressed against my throat. He was insane. I tried to talk to him slowly, very calmly. Then he raped me and slugged me and told me I must never try to leave his room.

"There was no way. He slept with the knife in his hand and if I so much as breathed heavily, he'd leap up. It was a filthy transient hotel. His door had three locks. So I played along. I'd dance in front of him nude, and he would watch my backside while he'd jerk off. He said he couldn't come any other way. I think that was why he raped women. While he was busy with himself I would study the locks. Then I told him that I wanted to be his old lady, that he was a great lay and we would work things out. It worked. The third day he finally turned his back on me. I must have opened those three locks in less than a tenth of a second.

"I made my way back to the Village. I wasn't thinking about the baby at all then. For the next three days I wandered around in a state of shock, I must have looked like Quasimodo. Bruised, beaten up, black eyes, they were so swollen I could barely see. Finally a friend spotted me. When he grabbed my arm, I flipped and started screaming. He got the rest of my friends together. They were all black. Most of them were from my home town. They considered me like

their little sister because in Baltimore—it was before
the black/white thing got heavy—I used to be very
friendly with a lot of black people. I gave them the
guy's name. He was in an Afro-Cuban band and his
name was on these promotion pictures he had all over
the walls. It was a freak thing—one of my friends
knew the guy. They went up to Harlem and took care of
him. They brought me back a cigar box. I didn't have
the courage to look in it. They just handed it to me
and said, 'He'll never do that to another girl again.' "

*

The young woman's aspirations were solidly and
pathetically upward-mobile, middle-class, prewomen's
lib American. What she lacked was discipline. She
wanted so desperately to be loved, it literally almost
killed her. By the age of sixteen she had run away
three times. In an attempt to control her, and excuse
themselves, her parents packed her off to the Anderson
School in Hyde Park. Private and expensive it was, but
she saw it as an expensive private prison. For $7,200,
parents of "mildly emotionally disturbed" students
can send them away to the Anderson School for a full
year.

Her pregnancy was no accident.

Counselors in contemporary abortion clinics who
see many such adolescent girls, before and after they
become prostitutes, have made some striking observations. An early, violent, usually incestuous sexual experience is common in the background of such girls.
"Absent parents"—either literally not present or in
any sense of love and nurturing absent—are another
common experience. The result is a girl who reaches
out for love through pregnancy. It is not thought out;
she does it on impulse. Behind her actions the counse-

lors generally discover one of two fantasies: either she hopes to create one person who *must* love her, owing to a baby's natural dependency, or she is seeking to re-enter her own childhood—to replace the emptiness by becoming a child again.

*

"When my boy friend found out I was not at boarding school, he hitchhiked up from Baltimore and waited for me at the Café Figaro. One day I walked in. He immediately got the rest of the money for the abortion. I was pretty far gone by then. Plus I had gonorrhea. But I didn't know it, all I knew was I burned and dripped. When I went to the hospital and told them about the rape and mentioned gonorrhea, the doctor laughed. He said it was only vaginitis, it would go away—and yes, I was four and a half months' pregnant.

"First we went to the heart of Pennsylvania coal country, to old Doc Spencer. Everybody knew about him. People from all over the United States came to Dr. Spencer for abortions. If you were poor, he wouldn't charge you. He did it out of compassion. By then he was an old, old man. I remember his examining room—the walls were covered with souvenir shop mottoes. But Dr. Spencer wouldn't touch me. He insisted I was too far gone. Six months, he said.

"I managed to get from there to Philadelphia and that night I took a train to South Philly. I had one more name, a black doctor who would do it for $600. The instructions were to wait in the train station around the bookstands. Three other girls were already there looking at books. We stood in the South Philly train station twirling and twirling those bookstands; none of us said one word. Then a man came over.

'Anyone for Dr. Bass?' he said. Suddenly there were three gasps of 'yes' and me.

"The driver took the money up front. We all sat in the doctor's waiting room in white johnny coats, like ghosts. He did all four abortions in an hour. When your name was called, the nurse just said, 'Up in the stirrups.' No anesthetic. The doctor went up inside with an instrument and told me to push. It was painful as hell. I remember the pressure building up. He said, 'Squeeze, push, squeeze, push,' and then he pulled and the baby came out. I heard it hit. He had one of those curved pans, like an ear. I remember seeing the baby very clearly. At four and a half months they're partly unwound. It looked like a little baby boy. It was perfectly formed, except for all the little things—the fingernails and the ears—and then the doctor packed me and I was back in the train station.

"The bleeding wouldn't stop. Three days later I removed the packing and the placenta came out. The pain was terrible. By the time my friends got me to Knickerbocker Hospital I was screaming, hemorrhaging—I was as red as your dress. The intake nurse took one look and said 'Murderess, you're a murderess!' When the doctor heard this he came right in. They told me later this nurse had had several miscarriages; I felt sorry for her.

"The doctor couldn't do a thing without my parents' permission. He called them. My father said yes, continue the abortion. Finally it became clear why old Doc Spencer had thought I was six months' pregnant. At Knickerbocker Hospital they delivered the second baby."

*

My eyes were drawn to her hands. Deep in the grain

of the backs of her hands swam dark purple tadpole shapes. Without thinking, I asked if she had been bitten by an animal.

A broken word rose in her throat. She fought it back and sat on her hands. Silent, caught. Eventually she was able to say those were her battle scars—the blood vessels burst by heroin needles, when the only uncollapsed veins she had left were in her hands. For four years in California she had been an addict with her husband, a hippie. He pushed dope and she supported his habit by hooking. I suggested this was a common, fatal trap in the sixties, by which manipulation masqueraded for love. She said she knew that now. She had left her husband and the cheap flesh market of Los Angeles with nothing but the clothes on her back. That was two years ago. She still loves him.

Today she is determined to build a good book in New York. Her goal is to chin up the social ladder toward a rich husband. By now she has assembled a $6,000 wardrobe, paid off most of her furniture, and has almost "done her teeth." The apartment belongs to another working girl who is living with a client in Italy. The address, the chandeliered lobby, the patina of hand-polished bronze elevators—all these things are critical if one is to maintain a champagne clientele. But she pays off no one. (Once a girl begins paying off, there is no end to the overhead.) In the interest of discretion, she allows no more than five of her most distinguished clients per week past the nosy doorman. Most of her call girl friends take an expensive exercise class at Kounovsky's gym and have maids. Not this one. The maids in her laundry room call her "Miss Do It Yourself." Hence she has collected six Sant'- Angelo gowns on sale, several hundred dollars worth of perfumes and body oils, and she is working on a mink. Save, save, save is her motto.

What she wanted when she first left home was a husband and a baby. What she got was a junkie with whom she couldn't have children. Now that she has had a taste of independent high living on $600 to $1,000 a week, her sights have been raised. She wants to hit the top as a call girl. She keeps telling herself it is the true liberation. There is only one thing missing— in her two years in New York she has not seen or held a man for anything but business.

*

"I had a monkey in California. She was so darling, very tiny. I made her a little pearl-knit sweater out of a man's sock. When I took her to the zoo everybody would follow me around. She didn't even dig the other monkeys.

"I love children. I'm a Jewish mother to everyone who knows me. I'd give anything to have a baby but number one, I don't know if I can succeed. After the rape, the gonorrhea, the botched-up abortion . . . and I have tried to get pregnant with two men since. Nothing happened. My husband, well, I always thought he was sterile. He was blocked with scar tissue from having V.D. many times. After I left him—he cut his hair and took a job. Without me around to support his habit, he kicked. Then he married a girl with two children of her own.

"Just recently he wrote that his wife was pregnant.

"Even if he wanted me, I could never go back to him. We'd fall right into the old heroin trap. In California you have to live with a man five years to become his common-law wife. We only made four and a half. But I still call him my husband.

"I wish I had another monkey."

*

I am thinking of a madam much older than this woman who began with the same dreams. We met during another Christmas season, in Manhattan Criminal Court. Beside the madam sat a richly furred dowager with eyes dull as rice grains. For want of amusement, it seemed, she had charged the madam with attempting to steal her Christmas packages in Lord & Taylor's ladies' lounge; the madam silently paid the fine. Then she invited me to her apartment to meet, as she phrased it, the one thing in this whole stinking world she could love and trust.

The Siamese cat had no claws. His teeth had been filed blunt. He had no use for claws or teeth, the madam assured me; she never lets him out and shuts him away when her clients come up. He was hers, all hers. Pimps have mean fists and lesbians scratch in fits of jealousy, she said. She sank gingerly into a chair and coddled one arm in the other as though, at one time or another, every cell of her skin had been violated. The cat did not spring into her lap. He was as defenseless as she. The cat paced, circled, studied his approach and leaped deftly over the chair back. Flirtatiously, then possessively, he wound himself around the madam's neck. In unison they purred. When she rose to make tea, the cat remained affixed to her neck. Even their eye movements were synchronized, as one might imagine a row of creature eyes behind dark bushes on an invaded island. I stared at the two until they became as one. A satyr born of mutual distrust. The perfect couple.

The liberated call girl is talking again: "My specialty is having just as good a time as my trick. That way I avoid going the lesbian route. I don't make as much money as other call girls, of course—the ones who are typically cold and calculating about the money. Most working girls want a forty percent cut for introducing you to one of their Johns. They come right over and get it before you go to sleep. But all my Johns are good friends. And if I'm busy I want them to have a good time with the best working girl I know. It's all a way of building a solid John Book. In a few years—"

Her phone is ringing. "Really, baby? And then his wife wanted him when he got home, beautiful!" She cups her hand over the receiver and explains this is her "boss." A former trick, a highly placed TV executive with a bachelor apartment on East 57th Street, he fakes as her employer whenever she needs a reference. "Last night he invited me and my girl friend over to do a sixty-seven-year-old judge. We had to pretend we thought he was a banker. We served him cold cuts, had a few giggles and hugs. He made it with both of us in the space of fifteen minutes. Then he went home to his wife and—well, you heard."

While she finishes talking, I flip through her magazines. *Playboy, Harper's Bazaar, Camera 35*, predictable—but what was this one with the cover torn off?

"Oh, that's some dopey women's lib thing."

Thinking this a quaint reverse on the cloth-covered porno novels one sees being guiltily devoured in the subway, I ask, "Are you interested in women's liberation?"

"That crap. I believe the man should always be the boss. A woman's place is one step behind him. She'll get her laurels through her husband's devotion. I know I feel feminine and secure in a man's arms—and a man feels more secure when a woman feels that way."

Again, her phone rings. "Really, sweetheart, it still aches?" She smiles cunningly. "Well, why don't we just fix that. Somewhere like Little Dix Bay?"

She hangs up ecstatic. "Whoopee, my travel business is really building up!" Humming, she looks over her cruise wardrobe.

In the past year she has begun to build a travel book of married real estate magnates and conservative politicians who invite her to Washington, D.C., Las Vegas, Houston. This is next to the peak position for a call girl. Traveling on the fatherly arm of handsome chairmen-of-the-board figures is not only fun, the rate is $500 a day (not including plane fare and hotel). One figures the maximum one would make at home taking all one's calls.

"And after all, you have to have brains and class as well as looks for the guy to want to spend twenty-four hours a day with you."

What about Little Dix Bay? I ask.

"We'll have a cottage together for two weeks in March. It's a celebration! Now this guy is really poor, but his company goes public this month. He'll be a millionaire for the first time in his life. So I'll do him a favor and give him a package deal. He's fun, he's easy to do, never more than twice a day. And it'll be a chance for me to learn scuba diving. I'll probably give him the whole package for $3,000."

Frowning: "If I charged him the normal rate he wouldn't be a millionaire for long."

Brightening: "And I'm looking to build a lasting clientele!"

The pinnacle of success, as the liberated call girl

describes it, is to meet a sugar daddy who will set her up for $50,000 a year in a duplex, in exchange for exclusive rights. The game has not changed at the top. Such men exist today in dwindling numbers, but the movie and cosmetic kings who do keep mistresses often keep several girls simultaneously.

"Right now I'm trying to meet one of the richest men in America. He keeps ten different girls in New York and I really respect him. He takes all the precautions, private detectives, tapping your wires, the works. Mmmmmmm—it makes you feel so secure."

*

Reality rarely serves the dream. The most beautiful playgirl may indeed land in the most lavish penthouse being kept in truffles and Porthault towels by a movie mogul—but that is not the end of the story. The torments that brought buyer and seller, sadist and masochist, together to begin with chew quickly through the curtains of make-believe.

A schoolteacher turned call girl worked her way up through a Supreme Court judge to the chief executive of a major movie company. She was the marvel of all her working girl friends. He installed her in a garden apartment. He openly displayed her in those bistros where prominent men who are anxious about their penis power display such things. He bought her a mink coat. He bought her a mink coat so that he could take it away whenever they had a fight. It became a game.

With a man like this, a working girl often begins drinking heavily. They went out every night. Then the schoolteacher began having nightmares. Sleep was impossible. She began gobbling barbiturates on top of the booze. One night very late the movie mogul barged in drunk. He wanted to play the game. But his playmate was deep in a drug-leaden sleep under the mink coat. He dragged her into the street and broke up her face with his fists and left her in the gutter.

In Bellevue's Psycho Ward she could not make the doctor understand. She was not a gutter case, she had a garden apartment. She moved with rich and famous people. This was all a terrible mistake. She would sue.

The doctor handed her a mirror. She couldn't look at the face. They asked her for identification. She told them to look in her mink coat. The doctor wrote on her chart "paranoia with delusions."

*

"The most beautiful working girl I know phoned last week—she had decided on suicide. She used to go with Sinatra, Eddie Fisher, all sorts of celebrities. If I had one-eighth of her looks, I could make a million. But she began living with a young guy and he broke it off. That's the way it happens.

"She called me up to say good-bye. She said she had already made reservations in a hotel where I wouldn't be able to find her. I didn't know where to begin. But I knew she'd go out in style. She wouldn't do it in a dingy place like the horrible little hotel where she was living with this guy. She'd do it in the Waldorf or the Plaza or the Drake. Money was no problem for her. She'd take a room for one night, go upstairs, eat a hundred Tuinals and go to sleep and die.

"I called all three hotels but she wasn't registered. Her old roommate hadn't heard from her in days. Suicide wasn't a new thing for this girl. She had ripped herself open so many times, she'd had to have plastic surgery just to stay in business. Such an exquisite girl

217

—we figured she was already dead.

"That Saturday afternoon her boy friend called me. He said he was too embarrassed to go out in the street and stop her. She was on the corner of Ninety-third Street in her underwear slicing her wrists with a razor blade."

*

If boy friends are a problem for the call girl, husbands can be a disaster. There are some prostitutes clever enough to manage the double life, but it requires absolute silence about their work. The only time a husband wants to hear about her clients is when a girl is trapped with a freak. In that case, the husband is generally delighted to rush over and break every bone in the man's body. Then he can say "I told you so."

The husbands of call girls are often terribly pretty, uncontrollably violent, luxury-loving gigolos. In other words, they are the penthouse counterpart of the street pimp. But the circles they move in dictate a different style. The gigolo husband often has a token job, selling men's clothes or doing cabinetry work for well-connected friends. His collection system is nothing so shaky as trailing his girl night after night by car. He controls her assets by marriage. When it comes to weaponry, he is also way ahead of the street pimp. It is not necessary to use brute force. His is the quiet power of blackmail.

The liberated call girl's best friend wanted a divorce. It had taken her several years to gather the courage to ask her gigolo husband. He had run through her bank account, sold her house in Florida, sold her Corvette. There was no ugly emotional scene when she asked for freedom . . . He simply stole her John Book.

He didn't demand outrageous sums. He would select an older married John, drive out to his home, and in the presence of his wife accuse the man of stealing a Cartier watch from a call girl. No ordinary mortal is prepared to explain his way out of such a charge in front of his family. Thus the gigolo husband collected $1,000 from each of six names, left a half-dozen men permanently miserable, and demolished his wife's career.

He then amiably granted her a divorce.

*

"My girl friends in the business say, 'I don't understand how you can like it. I hate it, hate the work.' And I say, 'Well, honey, you love your husband. You can't expect to be sexually attracted to anybody else, so to you working is a drudge.' But I don't have a husband. I don't even have a boy friend living with me. My Johns have to be my lovers and my friends. But you must understand—I really try to *help* these people.

"Yes, I'm used a lot. Men are using me for my body and to *my* Johns $100 means less than dirt. But I'm using them as much as they're using me. I'm paying my rent with them. And I get paid without getting involved.

"If I need somebody . . . I can take it from a professional basis to a personal basis. Like last week, I was dying to get out of town. When one of my favorite clients came over for his regular half-hour, I made it into an evening that I wanted. We drove to Monticello. After the races we had a romantic dinner, laughed, talked to one another—really talked—then we spent the night together. It was just like being in love.

"I only charged him for his normal half-hour.

"Some women can get married four or five times, but they're callous people. When I love, I'd lay my life down on the railroad tracks for the man."

*

What you really are, I said, is the perpetual victim.

The liberated call girl picked at the purple shapes imbedded in her hands.

"I know."

Chapter Nine

The call girl we've just met struck her bargain with life at the age of sixteen. The difference between the call girl and the courtesan we now meet comes down to one word. Discipline. This courtesan had the discipline to wait twenty years more, which allowed her to find, marry and survive . . .

THE ULTIMATE TRICK

The widow was not fat but overripe. While caretakers stabbed at the frozen February earth to prepare his final bed, she stood the overseer, at the topmost window of his country home, pulsing with life—her cheeks flushed (though briefly tear-streaked)—ready as a pear to drop from a tree. She was young.

Over one hundred guests were expected. It was a three-hour drive from the funeral home in Manhattan. That the snowfall would make the drive unpleasant for them was not what she was thinking about. For they were all respectably rich people with limousines and chauffeurs and lap robes. And the widow, although recently very, very rich, was not respectable. All that would change beginning today; today she was sole owner and chatelaine of Jumping Bluff. The coun-

try home which had been his greatest indulgence
would serve now as her launching platform; her affidavit. And so, standing at the window of the tower room,
she was engrossed in taking a slow, self-satisfied inventory:

Countless bolts of napped velvet lawn . . . fifty rare
paired trees incorporating the variety of a botanical
ark . . . twin man-made ponds, their breasts blackened
to give the illusion of infinite depth . . . the stable with
his and her Arabians and a Welsh pony for the children . . . a trout stream stocked with—how many trout
had he told her? No matter, it was as casually crowded
as a Woolworth's goldfish tank.

Placement of the more recent sculpture had been
under her direction. It was artfully scattered through
several acres of pine woods for the startled discovery
of guests: a prized David Smith, companion Henry
Moore nudes, the requisite Giacometti, and the newest, her fortieth birthday gift—one of Jean Tinguely's
mad machines. She smiled. With its iron arms, it was
once again blithely beating itself to a pulp. Her edict
that the mechanism be repaired overnight had been
followed. All was in order toward her plan. After the
funeral she would invite his most prestigious friends
and associates back to the house. It would appear, of
course, impromptu.

From here her eyes roved possessively over the sea.
Over her three-quarter-moon of beachfront. And on
around the headland seeking out the cleft in the bluff
that marked this stretch of the eastern Long Island
Coast, even amid the monotony of wealth, as a show-
place. But the bronze door in the face of the cliff was
not visible. Suddenly the clinging snow registered. It
was in her way.

She made a mental note to have the caretakers

remove the snow from the ornate bronze door; behind it lay an underground art gallery. This she would insist on showing the guests. A dizzying labyrinth of passageways, a luminous realm with the illusion of unreality, it doubled as a bomb shelter. It was like him.

Eccentric, cerebral, fabulous, monstrous—the chairman of the board of his own giant mutual fund—he had hidden deep within the gallery a splendid Raphael fresco. It depicted the beautiful nymph Galatea being vainly pursued by Polyphemus. It could be found only by those who grasped the lesson of the painting and of its position with respect to the other passageways, a lesson he had put to successful test in business life, and one that she too apparently had absorbed: To arrive at the ultimate goal one must first walk *away,* not directly toward, the treasure.

The widow found herself chuckling. A picture leaped to mind of the Chairman's brother, equally the tycoon in assets but conventionally stuffy in his style, as he stood beside her a few months before when the underground gallery was first opened. At the Raphael he openly gaped. "Only my brother could live like this," he said.

"Webb!"

She called out to a leathery man striding down from the gatehouse, the chauffeur. More than a chauffeur really, he was the long-standing butler/specialty chef /personal valet around Jumping Bluff, or what the Chairman, being English-born, always called "my man." The widow had inherited him.

"Come right up," she summoned. "I have a crash program for this morning." Already her voice had assumed the tone of sole command. The chauffeur looked up, but without stopping.

The funeral was at three. That left her six full hours, but she was miffed at the chauffeur for not moving faster. She looked forward to this morning's tour.

The widow was a woman given to recollections. Not of the flabby, sentimental sort. Reflections as a diligent exercise in reviewing her path to the present, about which she had been from earliest childhood lucid as plate glass. She was anxious to visit each room, to recall the private history it held, to relive the mute truths behind these walls that would remind her of how she came to be the Chairman's wife and mistress of his thirty-two-room estate. No one knew.

The tower crowned the classical Italian Renaissance house. It was the solitary tenant of the fourth floor. She knew every bitter inch of this room, its rigid verticals, the shadows that gathered in its vaulted ceiling, its elevated maiden's canopy bed . . . so many chaste weekends spent in that ridiculous bed. This was the room in which she had been forced to endure the first year of their arrangement.

At that time, while the house was being done, he had already taken on his first resident duchess: the decorator. Or to be more precise, the decorator had established the style of the house and thus incorporated herself into its being. She supervised the gardeners, planned the menus, personally combed the East End for seafood delicacies, and presided each weekend over the many guests as his hostess. In its first year, she was the life force of Jumping Bluff.

Over one critical area the decorator had not had control. He issued the invitations. When among the guests in his limousine on Friday evenings a younger woman began to appear, the decorator, for obvious reasons, dispatched her to the tower.

The irony was that this induced separation set the

pattern for their married life that made it all work. The Chairman could pride himself on the perpetuation of his total independence while his young wife could freely entertain a lover now and then, since she never visited his apartment in New York and he never intruded on her weekday life in the country. The couple co-habited only on weekends.

The tower turned out to be, so to speak, the decorator's drop zone. While she was looking to it for safety, the widow put a hole in her parachute. Now the widow was free to see the wild humor in it. She was laughing when the chauffeur's entrance caught her short.

"Well, isn't the mistress merry." He surveyed the widow with a knowing grin, then quickly added to mitigate his impudence, "What can I do for you this morning?"

"Hurry," she answered.

"Where do we start?"

"In his room." The widow passed the chauffeur in the doorway, beginning to dictate the list of odd jobs, and stopped. She noticed for the first time that he was not in uniform. He was turned out in a suede jacket, checkered slacks and a turtleneck sweater, a sweater black as his hair. The appealing result was not lost on her.

For a moment she reserved the judgment of an employer and considered him as a man: a robust Hungarian, exactly as tall as she but much darker, with blunt, brooding features. He was an educated person. A refugee. Perhaps that was why she had allowed him to drive her around town for her kinkier diversions, trusting him instinctively to be discreet. But those were trips she preferred to forget. She decided this was not the day to deal with the chauffeur.

"You'll be dressing properly later?" she inquired evenly.

"Of course." He closed the tower door after them. "The caretakers don't know what they're doing, I've been with them at the gravesite since dawn."

She thanked him and without further discussion led the way down the marble steps toward the Chairman's bed-study.

This morning the widow was drifting in in a particularly dreamlike state, the chauffeur observed. He could not take his eyes off her. She had become for him an exquisite moving part inseparable from Jumping Bluff . . . from its densely carpeted floors, ornamental columns, massive tables, soft-paste porcelain vases, majolica dinner plates, crystal chandeliers . . . and the vast, brilliant mirrors in which he had so long and quietly savored her passing reflection. She moved like a queen.

Her upbringing had prepared her for all this, but not in the way her acquaintances assumed. She was raised on a farm outside Richmond and could hardly lay claim to aristocratic stock. The secret was, she was a by-product of her mother's career as a pet realtor of men and women born into Southern privilege. At her mother's heels, she had acquired her taste and manners from observation of those clients and the closest inspection of their homes. All those Saturdays and Sundays of sweeping through Virginia's beautiful old country houses, caressing the English antiques as other children might fondle animals at the pet store, choosing from these showings *her* house—quite forgetting they were shopping for someone else—had awakened in the girl, very early, a lust for wealth.

In reality the financial picture was grim. In some

dim year of babyhood her father had disappeared.

As her own home had not prepared her for Jumping Bluff, neither had college trained the widow for her life's work: Pleasing rich men, providing them a perfect hostess, listening. (It was a wise girl friend who counseled her, "The great, great quality of successful courtesans is the ability to ask a question and listen to a man's answer as if your life depended on it.") After public school, she entered an obscure women's college as a fine arts major. The purpose was to develop her cultural background. Instead, she found the college full of excessively "nice" girls who were certain to marry ordinary men on schedule and find themselves at thirty-five with little to show for their labors but a seven-room house and stretch marks. She left in the middle of the first year.

So complete was their vicarious intake of the upper-class Southern tradition that the subject of college never came up again between mother and daughter. "Develop your wiles" was all her mother had to say.

Hence she had labored and studied and plotted and waited, and waited some more, resisting all temptations short of her goal, until she was—think of it!—thirty-six.

"I want you to look at the door on this armoire," she said, as the chauffeur followed her into the formal French bed-study. Here the Chairman had slept, breakfasted, read the morning papers, studied the market quotations, but rarely welcomed company—even that of his wife. She pointed to the Chairman's largest wardrobe.

The chauffeur gave one tug on the gilded handle and the door dropped from its hinges. The more he wrestled with it, the more absurd he began to look.

"I'm—sorry," he stammered, and finally set the door down. The two of them stood confronted with the dead man in silhouettes of a dozen vivid colors. Caught in the scent of his cologne.

"It's hard to find a man," she suddenly thought aloud.

"Not if you're looking for a real man," the chauffeur said, letting his breath come hard.

"He and I were ideally happy," she responded defensively. "You know why? We remained individuals. I let him remain exactly as he was from his boyhood."

"What else could you do with a monk for a bridegroom?"

"I'll tell you one thing. *All* men need a long rope." She drew away from the chauffeur, into herself, and began slowly circling the room. "I couldn't have had a more difficult man, I can tell you that," she said. "The most difficult man in the world."

"You had a few tricks up your sleeve." He turned back to the armoire and his work.

Scarcely aware of the chauffeur now, she stopped before each antique and observed it without touching, as if the room were a museum. It summoned memories of Perls. . . .

The object, after college failed her, was to taste the New York art world for herself. She selected out of the Madison Avenue galleries one of the most traditional, Perls. They habitually hired "secretaries" whose chief function was to be decorative—in the F.F.F. sense of decorative—that is, mildly animated versions of Fine French Furniture. The job gave her a chance to sit all day studying "the ladies." Perls drew its clientele from those Park Avenue matrons who, for lack of anything better to do, browse through the same old Rouaults and Dufys as dutifully as pushers of A & P carts. She studied them for every detail of marginal differentiation. The cut of shoes, the coat labels, the Long Island lockjaw pattern of speech that allowed them to stand before the work of a still risky contemporary artist, and to safely say: "I've never *hurrrd* of him, but isn't it amusing?" Or "raather fun." She trained her mind to think as they did. Before leaving Perls, she knew their lives, their preferences, their formula so well that their very instincts had become hers. She was the almost perfect facsimile.

Now stopping before the Chairman's Louis Quatorze bed, the widow ran her hand over the suede quilt. For a moment, she let the saline build up beneath her eyelids. Set out in their customary place, over a worn patch in the tea rose carpet, were her husband's velvet slippers.

"Why don't you let yourself have a good cry?" the chauffeur asked.

"Because I'm made the way I am," she said. "I'm regarded as very independent. I'll always be that way."

"Always?"

"That's right."

She gave him another job. A heavy painting was askew.

There were several portraits of her in the house, but this one had been the Chairman's favorite. She was leaning against a dark building in a ruby red dress, her throat and arms receptive as the funnels of spring lilies, her body very slim. It was before the children.

The Chairman had often tried to describe what so deeply attracted him to this portrait; it was not her youthful dimensions, he said. Sometimes in the night when she happened to pass his room, she would see him crouched at the foot of his bed, staring at it. These nocturnal adventures she never interrupted. If he preferred her in fantasy to the flesh, this too she was prepared to respect. The Chairman was a prude. Very early she had learned not to make demands on rich men that they couldn't satisfy. She didn't demand perfect behavior. In bed she never demanded, except to please. What she did demand, they could easily give ... gifts, trips, homes.

Of course, the widow knew exactly what the Chairman saw in the portrait. The painter, an Italian lover, had captured what first excited him: about her there was an indefinable quality—the compelling play of messages in her lip movements, some said—which beckoned men, unnerved women and was in the end profane.

The chauffeur gave a low moan. He was on a step stool, his arms wrapped around the painting. "You know what you are?" he said. "A goddamned medieval sorceress."

"There is that quality . . ." She didn't flinch at his profanity; he was stating a fact. "But I also have the naive directness, as it were, of one coming from the farms."

He stepped down from the stool. With his back to the widow, he stared at the woman in the painting. "You know what else? You're the only person I know who waves for a taxi just like a prostitute."

She stopped to wonder where he had seen her alone. Then she laughed.

"That disconcerted my husband, too. I've always been *ver*-ry direct. It's useful in keeping people unaware, because they don't expect me to look the way I do and be as direct as I am. Especially where profit is concerned, I get right to the point."

The chauffeur muttered something about it having been useful in Italy.

"What was that?" Her tone of voice instantly sharpened. "Speak up."

"I said," and he faced her now, "it must have been useful when you had your own business in Italy."

"The modeling business, you mean."

A beat.

"Of course. The modeling business."

He knew. And now they both knew that he knew. Well, what of it, the widow thought. "That was a long time ago and in another country, as they say," and she laughed as if at a trifle. Allowing herself a reverie of pure ego, she took her time leaving the room. . . .

After Perls', she had spent the next few years in Italy and France. She lived between the two countries out of several Vuitton cases while acquiring taste, objets d'art and cash. Lovers were an incidental item, though she attracted more than her share of ascetically tortured Italian artists and gaunt French novelists, and though she enjoyed them hugely, being a country girl of more than ordinary lust and no religious pretensions at all.

The best way to attract money, she had discovered, was to give the appearance of having it. This was a pure business matter. And so she organized a roving troupe of thin American girls who by day became prized as models. She couldn't model herself for a very simple reason. By some accident of genetics, the truth of her stock intruded on the fine-boned nobility of her frame in only one spot: she had big lush peasant breasts.

Management of the troupe was her natural role. By night her girls dispensed additional favors to a discerning clientele. It was strictly a cash and carry business. No middle men or madam, no address book per se, no strings on where her girls went or what services they chose to perform. As manager of the troupe she had only two rules, but they were immutable. Her girls were available only to men who paid by gift or cash for their entertainment. And all the gifts and cash were held by her for "safekeeping." In the event a girl had second thoughts about returning from a yacht party to meet her modeling commitments, she forfeited her nighttime bank.

The widow kept an apartment during that period in Ravenna, once the stronghold of Byzantine rule in Italy. One of her admirers always made bad jokes about "the American Empress Theodora." She would reply with the equally bad joke about laughing all the way to the bank. But she did, indeed, laugh a lot during those years. Her apartment was so filled with bibelots, it was like living over the bazaar.

During her stint in Ravenna she also remade herself in the Byzantine mold. She studied the frescoes. Except for the farm-girl breasts, she emerged the ideal copy: an extraordinarily tall slim figure with tiny feet, an almond-shaped face dominated (through artifice) by huge, staring eyes. To highlight the translucence of her skin she favored purples and blues. Her clothes were chosen not to deny, but to accentuate her verticality—"A master stroke," the Chairman acknowledged early in their courtship. Dressing each night for dinner in geometric patterns and dark thick velvets, she did carry off to perfection the mood of an empress in a mosaic. All this, and her ramrod posture, came from attentive study of the bodies in Byzantine art—bodies that seem to be capable only of slow, ceremo-

nial gestures and the display of magnificently orna-
mented costumes.

Ordinary men might have thought her dangerous.
But the Chairman was no ordinary man.

"By the way," the chauffeur broke into her thought,
"did you invite your Italian racing car magnate?"

"Yes."

"I didn't see his name on the guest list."

Her answer carried no trace of resentment. "I expect he was out of the country when my wire arrived."

This was one of the widow's two sterling character
traits. She was terribly circumspect; not only in the
way she dressed, gave her parties, ran her house, but
she never allowed herself a wicked tongue. And she
was not a whiner. In both Italy and France she had
warmed up several times for worthy marriages that
appeared certain, but in each case she suffered a near
miss. These were not brief liaisons. To each of these
men in turn she devoted daily warmth and pampering. They cost her a total of ten years. But when the
racing car magnate wouldn't marry her, she didn't
whine about it. Nor was there a whimper when things
didn't work out with the statesman, the French wine
king, the publisher. Everyone in her troupe gave her
credit for being a brick.

The problem was, eventually, her reputation. Approaching thirty-five, she was no longer convincing in
the fickle playgirl role floating around villas and
yachts. She was becoming an old face.

In Europe it looked to her girl friends as though she
would become an incorrigible courtesan. They sold
her short. One day, emphatically, she upped and came
back to New York, having decided it was the only
Imperial City left in the western world. Or at least, the

only one accessible to a girl of the farms.

Here, her small portable fortune collected in antiques and objets d'art stood her in good stead. It would take a while to re-establish herself in New York. Meanwhile, she accepted the role of mistress to several men in turn. She had houses by them—never children, the time wasn't yet right—and gave birth to dazzling interiors in places like Peapack, New Jersey, and Old Lyme, Connecticut. This was strictly a holding action. She always had resale value to fall back on.

It was a proud moment when one of these benefactors, a politician of whom she was particularly fond, proposed. She refused of course. The widow had never allowed natural instincts to deflect her from her ultimate goal. And by then, after thirty-plus years of study, the specifications of that goal were as clear in her mind as a page from Standard and Poor's. Not for her were men of transitory power, such as politicians. Nor was she even fleetingly seduced by paper millionaires whose assets were inevitably locked up in their own company's unstable stock. No, she had returned to New York with a specific sort of rich man in mind: one who already had entered that exclusive pantheon of the powerful, one whose influence was feared but acknowledged, one who came with an established address on Park Avenue, a country home, abundant servants and tax-free bonds. But most especially—he had to be free of heirs.

For a short, bleak period around her thirty-fifth birthday, she almost lost her nerve. Most of her old girl friends had settled for artsy craftsy sycophants who were attentive but broke. Others were having babies, breeding dogs, taking overdoses.

She could fix an exact date to the beginning of the Chairman's exclusive proprietorship. Christmas Eve, four years ago. It was a certain dinner party given by one of those bachelor sales executives in luxury businesses—this man was in furs—for the purpose of introducing tycoons to possible mistresses or wives. It was an old New York convention. The host would invite the beautiful new girls in town: models, actresses, the dumb but pretty daughters of Europe. The subplot of the party was, for every match made, the host sold a fur. The Chairman didn't hide the fact that he was aggressively bored. He left at ten. Someone mentioned his age was fifty-two and he had no heirs. But neither did he have the slightest use for women. The man was a virtual recluse. That made it even more delicious a challenge. She told the host she would want a sable coat when, not if, she married him.

"Will you have some flowers brought up for the children's rooms," the widow directed the chauffeur. "And make sure Mrs. Ryan takes them out after their breakfast."

Alone in her daughter's room, she rearranged the china animals and antique dolls displayed behind glass cases. Her daughter was three. She rarely played in her room.

The Chairman had been quite beguiled by the little girl, once she left the crib and became interested in what he had to say. Her special gift to her father was an unrestrained physical gaiety. She was forever somersaulting down the bluff in brightly flowered swimming suits, disregarding the protests of her nanny, bringing him back an incessant collection of shells. But she was not a boy.

One triumph always seemed to lead to another predicament; it had been hard enough work getting the Chairman to marry her. He more or less proposed quite early. She didn't have to show her hand. Then, like most men, he got cold feet.

"You have to take a stand as soon as you know you're in like Flynn," her mother had advised her. They kept in close touch by telephone. "As soon as you know a man's so comfy and cozy, he's gotten the habit of having you do all those little personal things, you must make your move. When he's happy to leave things just as they are—then, you up and show him you can live without him!"

The problem was, the Chairman felt about his fortune much the same way old panhandlers feel about their corner; it was his dominion. She could read him like a book. He was also concerned about jeopardizing his unchallenged authority over the company. Wouldn't his colleagues think him suddenly unstable for having fallen in love after so many years of seclusion? She planted in his mind the idea of a morganatic union. And then let him think on it for a year, without interference, until he came back with the offer as if it were his own.

Her education in these matters came from many trips to Versailles, where she had pondered the history of those mistresses who held their ground and those who fell away in humiliation. Her model was the Marquise de Maintenon, a country girl who became the most successful commoner in the court of Louis XIV. To begin, she earned a new name and title when the king admitted her to the court as a lady-in-waiting to his prevailing mistress. With his gift of 200,000 livres, meant to maintain her new status, she bought an estate in a spot called Maintenon, of which she became known as the marquise. When his queen died, with twenty years of philandering behind him, Louis was confident the modest Maintenon would consent to become his next mistress. But, as the widow read in historical accounts, "he found in her a politic restraint: it must be marriage or nothing." Maintenon was fifty when she achieved her goal. It was a morganatic union, a contract whereby the mate of inferior status acquires no new rank and no hereditary rights. Neither do the children have title to the property of the higher-ranking parent, but they are definitely considered legitimate. It worked for the Marquise de Maintenon. (Of course, at the urging of the king's counselors, the ceremony was not made public, and there are some who believe it never took place.) But to the widow's way of thinking, the contract probably exceeded the country girl's wildest expectations, being the only union whose vows the king appeared to have kept.

Three centuries later, the Chairman and his bride had enacted a near replica of French history. Excepting that the widow went the marquise one better. When she bore the Chairman an heir, only a year ago, he was delighted to the point of elevating their left-handed marriage. He granted his wife and children full inheritance rights. Shortly thereafter, in the presence of a few friends and close associates, for the first time he "brought her out."

More than any of her contemporaries in that rarified circle of women in the business of marrying rich men, she had dreamed the dream and made it work. The widow passed quickly through the room of her son, finding it in perfect order.

The chauffeur intercepted the widow on the stairs; a call had come in about the Chairman's brother.

"He's in the hospital with appendicitis," Webb reported. He allowed his voice to make no interpretation of the news.

"How awful," the widow said. "I was counting on him being here."

"You'll carry on. You always do."

"That's right." It was her most characteristic expression; beneath the emphasis on "right" echoed a rock bottom authority.

She hurried down the steps to inspect the main floor. All was under control in the kitchen. It was a heartless steel room devoted only to the mechanical, as are most kitchens of people rich enough not to be obliged to cook there. The breakfast room bulletin board was crammed with messages.

"What's this one from the Senator?" the widow questioned the chauffeur. "There's nothing but a number."

"I have the idea he might not show up," Webb teased her. "I think he's having an affair with a Samoan girl now, in Samoa."

"Well, I don't have much to say about the Senator," she lied. "When you think, he's so beautiful that every woman's going to fall all over him. There's really nothing more boring."

She launched into a spate of questions. Had the snow been removed from the art gallery door? Who was receiving the flowers? Were enough coming in to fill all the rooms or should they phone up to the greenhouse?

The chauffeur's deference flagged. "Where did you get the idea for this reception?" Distracted, arranging flowers, she took his remark as a compliment.

"I read history," she said. "And I *am* an intelligent woman."

"Shrewd," the chauffeur said, "but not intelligent."

"Oh well, what's the difference?"

"Intelligence is the ability to analyze." Webb stood side by side with her, working in the flower-cutting sink. "You can analyze only for yourself. And that's not intelligence, it's shrewdness."

"You read too much Proust," she said.

In the dining room the widow felt immediately close to the Chairman. How vividly she remembered the night he brought her out. . . . It was a testimonial dinner for the museum curator. Very formal, terribly intellectual. She had only recently given birth to the boy and was still full and milky in her post-partum state—a testimonial to the Chairman's "vigor" upon which everyone at the dinner table remarked. They were people to whom euphemisms came easily.

It occurred to the widow that she had enjoyed herself most in this room. Here she lived through her husband at his best. He was always an intellectual adventurer, an irreverent paterfamilias who loved to gather around him the few keenest minds in his company for a weekend of formal meals and brisk walks. Throughout the coveted weekends at Jumping Bluff, he would lecture these young fund managers whose task it was to run pools of money under tremendous pressure. They were, especially before the boy's birth, his surrogate sons.

She paused at the window behind his chair to stare at the portico; it was uncanny. So thoroughly dominant was his presence, she could feel him sitting down at the green cool marble table spread with shrimp and white wines. During lunch and dinner, he would sweep the same guests off on another trip through fresh realms of human affairs, transporting them with the incredible velocity of his mind. The children were never turned away. He would be discoursing brilliantly on the latest billion-dollar merger on Wall Street, on how the Street was the true battlefront of post-industrial Western man, the hunting ground of the imperial animal—when the audacious little girl would fly into his lap. Or the clinging boy would say "Gup? Gup, Daddy?" A moment later, the children included, he would be telling tales of ancient and modern Medicis or comparing a picaresque baron of the nineteenth-century railroad industry to a politician in the news . . . often ending his tales abruptly with a chuckle and the ironic comment . . . "And this is the human condition?"

She never said much; she learned. In these monologues he hovered always over history, swooping down on it to retrieve support for his theories with the deadly accuracy of a hunting hawk. No one argued with the Chairman.

In the classical tradition, leaving the men to talk business, she had always retired early from the dinner table. Wives of guests were expected to follow the custom. But where to take them had become a problem during that long period when she was re-doing the main salon. She had completely sealed it off. Not only because of disorder, but because it had come into being under the decorator's reign. It had been an all beige room . . . cool, minimally furnished, pure classical from its exquisite moldings to its collection of bronze dolphins. Not any more.

Today, although it was missing a few finishing touches, she would open the doors of her main salon for the first time. This was the project by which she had finally unseated the Chairman's former duchess. She thought of it as a labor of love.

In less elevated circles, where women who dispense

their favors for a payoff are called prostitutes, the widow's action could correspond to that of the scorned streetwalker who rushes out to smash her rival's apartment. The distinction again was patience. To dismantle the decorator's backdrop, the widow had taken three full years.

"Oooh, aren't they magnificent!"

Her sounds were happily girlish as the chauffeur heaped into the widow's arms all of the winter wildflowers he had found in the woods. "There's nothing like the natural," she said.

But as they set out the ordinary flowers in the extraordinary main salon, the widow began to fret. They weren't really appropriate . . . though it was original . . . she wasn't sure. . . .

"I do believe the mistress is nervous," the chauffeur said.

"We'll have the wildflowers in the foyer." She announced her decision with authority. After all, the wildflowers had been the chauffeur's idea. Today, welcoming her peers to Jumping Bluff, it was essential that everything reflect *her* taste, *her* wealth and power, her intention to actively administer the Chairman's estate and to discharge her position as a major stockholder in the firm. In fact, she already had a particular divorcé in mind as a possible—only possible—replacement for the Chairman. She asked the chauffeur to check that his name was on the reception list.

"Who's he?" the chauffeur asked, feigning ignorance.

"President of the Resort Fund, as you well know." She looked at her watch, turned away, and issued another flurry of commands.

He gave an odd, triumphant grunt. "You really think of yourself as the debutante widow, don't you?"

"Will you have the fire?"

Startled, she dropped her rings on the bathroom floor. It was only Mrs. Ryan, moving about the widow's bedchamber with her altogether colorless and efficient visage.

"Lovely idea," she answered. "I thought I'd have a short nap before the funeral. Will you bring the children?"

As the housekeeper was leaving, she called, "And a second breakfast?" adding the automatic "Thanksomuch."

The widow was occupied with adjusting the weights on her Modesto scale, a veritable fixture in the bathrooms of rich men's wives. The tilt was not flattering. She would have to get tough with herself. Hidden for three years miles out of action in Jumping Bluff, she had assumed the habit of retiring at eight with an after-dinner tray. For the first time in her life she began to fear the word "plump."

Even this the Chairman had not found disagreeable. In fact, there was nothing that pleased him more than to see her here in maternal repose. He often watched from the doorway while the children were tucked under the tapestry coverlet, one on either side of her like two suckling piglets, while she indulged herself on trays of oatmeal swimming in cream. He found it entirely sensual, he had said, to see her pampering his girl and breast-feeding his boy. This came as no surprise to the country girl. How often her mother had remarked, "A woman's greatest hold on a man is his children."

And so almost without exception, every weeknight

of their married life, she had retired to the fourposter with her TV guide and a stack of political science journals hiding muscle magazines. She always slept with the children.

"Ready or not, here I come!"

From the foyer came sounds of ferocious beasts. Then a trill of laughter from the little girl who sat bolt upright on her mother's bed.

"Unkie's here!"

The widow felt relieved. Every such household has an "Unkie" by one name or another; in this house he was not the lady's lover. He was the master's stage Englishman, an incorrigibly cheerful man of no known gainful employment. He sponged on the rich in exchange for performing various animal imitations and inserting fascinating trivia into formal dinner conversation. With a proper British accent.

"I'll be right down to go over the new guest list with you," the widow called from her bedroom. After the nap, she felt almost giddy. "We're having a reception!"

II.

The Italian stone lions at the entrance were covered with snow by the time the widow's car turned onto the gate road. The church was twenty minutes away.

"You're absolutely certain that Mother's driver will get her there on time?"

"I told him all my shortcuts, but you know these hired limousine companies," the chauffeur said. He wiped over the perspiring window of the Chairman's fudge brown Rolls Royce and lowered the window. There were two buttons for closing the window; the second operated at a slower speed, lest fingers be caught in the top. "Look at that *snow,*" he said.

The widow was busy adjusting her headpiece. Cursed with frizzy, lackluster hair, she always wore hats or falls. Today's was a particularly inspired head-dress, a helmet of black seed pearls with a drifting double veil. She wanted to solemnize her medieval look.

"On your left, cage of the live chauffeur," he announced. They were passing the stone gatehouse where he was quartered apart from the rest of the servants.

"You've nothing to complain about," she said. "Many's the time I've wished I could take a holiday alone in the gatehouse, picking wild flowers, watching for deer—"

"For sev-en-teen years?" Each syllable of his solitary duration was cut in stone. He ran his hand possessively over the Rolls' waxed mahogany dashboard. "This has been my real home."

The radiophone buzzed. The chauffeur lifted the speaker piece from its cradle on the floor.

"Mrs. Ryan? Webb here." While the housekeeper relayed a report that the widow's mother had been collected safely at East Hampton airport, the chauffeur toyed with the phone buttons. There were seven: one for Jumping Bluff, three for the airports and three for New York—the Chairman's office, his apartment, his club. Webb glanced at the gas gauge as they approached a Shell station.

"Will you be driving back to town tonight?" he asked.

"I haven't decided."

From the back seat came the sound of kid gloves being snapped against the palm of a hand.

Her driver turned decisively into the service station.

"No," she protested. "We haven't time!"

His insolence having now mounted to outright insubordination, the chauffeur ordered the tank filled. He did not speak again until they were back on the highway.

"I thought you might be in the mood for a little diversion tonight—" he paused, "on Forty-second Street."

"Don't be ridiculous," she snapped.

"Shall I call the office and have someone find out what's on at your favorite movie houses? I couldn't find any good leather and motorcycle numbers for you in today's paper—"

"Stop it," she commanded.

He would not stop it. This was his trump card. All the way to the church he tormented her with recollections of her trips to Times Square, of the many six-hour stretches he put in following her at a discreet distance through the vilest streets in his beautiful Rolls . . . how he wondered why she didn't care what the movie titles were . . . why she just wandered from one vulgar theater to another, indulging herself in uninterrupted pornography, eating popcorn up in the balconies alone. . . . "and why didn't you invite me along?"

"You bastard," she said.

He ignored her.

"I'm told there is a terribly tasteful homosexual gallery on Christopher Street," he continued. "Floor-to-ceiling pictures of very young, very clean, very well-endowed—"

The radiophone interrupted him. It was the housekeeper again, she had finally got through to the Senator's office. The widow brightened, until she heard the report.

"The Senator's sending flowers and his representative wants to know how to find the church."

The chauffeur began reciting elaborate directions. The widow broke in with one acid line.

"Just tell the *representative* to turn off Montauk at Hedges Lane."

This was a brand-new note in her voice, evident only in the past few days: urgency. After forty years of control, she *expected* what she wanted. The expectation showed perilously in her voice.

She was suddenly afraid. If her patience deserted her now, how would she deal with the chauffeur? She had come to think of him as repulsive but benign. It would not have occurred to her to see him as a pimp figure, waiting his chance to compel a woman to support him. It came as a gathering shock that he, in the end, was more disciplined than she.

"Too bad about the Senator," he said, without a trace of remorse.

"I'm not shopping for a prince consort."

"You don't have to. You already have one."

He took off his hat.

The Chairman had played his fund managers like a cast of puppets. He was a virtuoso at making them dance to the throb of their competitive juices, taking care over the years that their feet should never touch the ground more than fleetingly. With the master's death, the sudden vacuum created a rush of freedom that had affected these men like too much oxygen on a mountaintop. They had all gone a bit mad.

Even now, safely sealed in their limousines clique by clique, the fund managers and main executive officers were flagrantly politicking for power before the old man was in the ground. When these exchanges grew sticky, the conversations switched with nearly equal enthusiasm to gossip. For even to these close associates and their wives, closer to the dead man than his friends, the Chairman's private life had been a constant bafflement.

It was only by reading the obituary that they had learned the dates of the children's births and the marriage—some didn't even know he had a wife. There was a great deal of talk on the drive to Amagansett.

Covetous talk . . .

"From the little I've seen, she seems like an easygoing person."

"She has reason to be easygoing."

Salacious talk . . .

"How much did she sell that big baby for?"

"It was a Renoir, and it was a million and a half, or maybe a million six—"

(The conversation in this car was between the company's pet salesman, a coarse but talented man, and an executive secretary.)

Salesman, whistling: That's gelt. Did she have it out here or in the city?

Secretary: Out here in her house. It was a birthday gift.

Salesman: Really, does she stay at whatchacallit all year?

Secretary: Jumping Bluff. Most of the time. (The secretary's voice level dropped.) Except when she feels like seeing her contacts in New York.

Salesman: Great! Hey, does this broad need a lover? Tell her I'll be right over.

Only one person was in the know—the decorator—the woman who had preceded the widow in the dead man's belated affections. A long lean tulip of a woman, the decorator was particularly admired for that marvelous thistle of a voice that makes English secretaries so highly prized and which under no circumstance carries a note of alarm. Her traveling companions belonged to the "friends" category: A college trustee, a California industrialist and his wife, an art dealer—but not being "close business associates," they were quite uninformed about the dead man. A pair of skis laid over the seat bisected their numbers, since the art dealer was going straight from the funeral to a skiing holiday. They were not what one would call a deeply mournful group.

And so in the decorator's car, curiosity got the better of diplomacy. She was virtually interrogated. They all wanted to know. . . . Why did the man marry after barricading himself in a luxurious bachelorhood for well over half a century?

The decorator took pleasure in releasing her answers like a well-baited casting line. In high-flown parables she described this imperial man: how he had fought and conquered the armies of Wall Street, risen by his wit on the shoulders of his enemies, assumed rule of a company worth two billion dollars in mutual funds, acquired generous quantities of stock and extended his reach with a TV station, and how he had then accepted a string of honorary degrees bestowing influence over and above his robes of power. Fifty was the number his life was all about. Only when he made that deadline, by casting himself at the age of fifty as Chairman of the Board of his own company, could the man let up on himself. The decorator stopped, withdrawing the bait while she lit a cigarette. They bit.

"What else could he possibly have needed?" the industrialist's wife demanded. "And why did he choose her?"

Having in his later years bought several homes, the decorator continued, and having surrounded himself with servants and a stunning art collection, he had nothing left to prove in a man's world. Except the power of his physical equipment. At the age of sixty-three, with the birth of his first child, a young wife endowed him with virility.

"But why did *she* marry *him?*" the men wanted to know. To avoid being thought petty, the decorator took a long pause to lend her short answer full emphasis.

"Could it be the obvious?"

Abruptly, at the steps of the church, each clot of arriving guests dropped its chatter and donned the veils of reverence. The decorator greeted the widow with all the gestures of deep bereavement; they left a few sobs behind one another's ears, discussed the flowers, linked arms and confronted the altar with the implacable dignity of porcelain birds. On the widow's other arm was the stage Englishman. No widow could hope to be accompanied by two people more attentive to proper form. Moments before they led her down the aisle, the Englishman remembered to drop the veil over her helmet.

On one side of the aisle sat a long line of aging freckled men with hawkish noses, the company's surrogate sons and elderly women in practical snow boots —it was the Chairman's side. Opposite sat the widow's two mad, satin-doused aunts, looking like twin Elsa Lancasters, and her freewheeling girl friends—a contrast that was visibly bizarre.

The funeral had to wait for her mother.

Directly behind the widow was the divorced wife of the president of the Resort Fund. The widow had seated the president at a prudent remove from herself, since he was the man she expected to inherit along with her late husband's stock in the company.

The president of the Resort Fund would be the Board's obvious choice to replace him.

An usher had seated the company arbitrageur next to the divorcée. A deeply diplomatic man, he had noted her husband on the opposite side of the aisle and was fumbling with polite inquiries. Their conversation was the result of that sudden, uncomfortable intimacy into which business associates are thrust at weddings and funerals. Wouldn't she prefer he exchange seats, there must be some mistake. . . .

"There's no mistake. We're divorced."

"Oh, I'm sorry."

"Don't be. He left me quite comfortable."

"Really, I didn't know. I mean, I don't know anything about his background . . ."

"His family was all Lafitte Rothschild and escargot. They had Matisses before anyone heard of Matisse."

"How fortunate. Well, it sounds as though you've both been quite civilized about the split."

"*Civilized?* My husband has been going to an analyst five days a week for three years."

"Good, it will probably help him get better."

"Oh, no," she said, her voice hollow as a waiting tomb. "He'll never get better."

The delay had become an imposition by the time the widow's mother arrived. Yet judging by the murmur that hummed through the pews as the strange country lady from Virginia was seated, the wait had been worth it. She wore a purple snood, floppy beige boots and an expression one could only call nakedly acquisitive. The whispers mounted.

"That's her *mother!*"

The coffin was covered with limp white tea roses.

250

The snow had not stopped. Everyone had trouble parking.

The guests on the reception list all had been contacted on the steps of the church by the stage Englishman and the decorator. They were urged to come back to the house for a buffet, for the evening, to wait out the snow, to stay overnight if they wished. But to be on the safe side, the widow expressed again her hospitality to people in the front row around the Chairman's family mausoleum. They were all standing ankle deep in snow. Above them the evergreens too were mourning, under their fresh white topping.

The chauffeur recorded that for a brief moment over the casket the widow openly wept. Then the enormous eyes dipped into the deep recesses above her puffed cheeks. Staring at the gravesite, her face looked robbed.

The ceremony was over.

Old people grunting as they folded over and tucked themselves back into limousines, old men with their sparse hair pasted over a lost part, old men's eyes slack in their sockets, turning away from proof of their own mortality—this is what the widow saw through her blowing black veil as she turned from the grave. She reached for the hands of the rector and the curate. The moaning of snow tires could already be heard.

Led single file by the chauffeur, a long line of highshouldered Cadillacs joined in the recessional, leering through the pine woods with their fog lights dulled to yellow smiles. Their haunches were mud-spattered and snow-dirty, almost tacky. The chauffeur was about to observe how thin is the veneer of dignity even over immense wealth. He decided to say nothing more for the moment. The widow was adjusting her veils when their car turned down the hill toward the house.

The chauffeur alone saw, in his rear view mirror, that the guests' cars were turning the other way.

Toasty smells drifted from the dining room, where creamed meats waited cradled in silver chafing dishes. The stage Englishman and the decorator were the first two guests who came back to the house. The decorator came because she was something of a courtesan herself. And despite their contretemps over the Chairman, she had always been temperamentally drawn to the widow. The stage Englishman came because he loved gossip and parties. They were followed by the widow's mother and two maiden aunts.

Feverishly gracious, the widow welcomed them into the main salon. It was a moment sweet with triumph. She was not only displaying the room for the first time, she was showing it off for the benefit of the decorator. To unseat her had meant dismantling piece by piece the furnishings into which the decorator had integrated herself, and taking great pains to redo everything in heavy, medieval colors—beginning with the custom-made velvet wall coverings.

"I adore it," her mother gushed. Moments later, she and the aunts were deliberating how to "liven it up." They made their way upstairs and selected their favorite guest rooms, to occupy more or less permanently beginning with the next trip. Back in the main salon the mother gave a blanket invitation to the two other guests for imagined dances and dinner parties of the future. The two aunts gave a bad performance of comforting the bereaved, while remarking with undisguished covetousness on the wall coverings.

"It's certainly an individual expression," the decorator said finally of the main salon. "It's you."

Beyond that, she was at a loss for words. It was a room of smoky mirrors and antique satin sofas, long, very long sofas glutted with bolsters and pale boudoir pillows, a gilt harpsichord—a room not only shamelessly indulgent but truly whorish. The decorator made herself a stiff drink.

The doorbell was not ringing. The widow's eyes were dangerously tired.

All at once, sitting in the virtually empty main salon, the widow felt it impossible to keep up her blind conversations with five people a moment longer. Her mind was disobediently scanning the guest list, the names of those who said they would come back after the interment, but didn't, the names of those who never came at all. Fortunately, her mother felt apprehensive about getting to the airport in the snow. Minutes after her relations left, the widow rose abruptly.

"I think the snow is on all our minds. I'd feel better if you two went on and let me wait for the other guests."

It was dark. She walked outside with the decorator and the stage Englishman, preserving form to the last, and then she turned back to the gaunt, echoing house. It was not going to happen. All those years consumed in the preparation and execution of the perfect match, thinking herself so discreet, so well-protected, with nothing but a possibly treacherous servant to fear— and now they both were to be deserted. The legacy of position alone was not enough; she hadn't figured on that. People respected power and the Chairman's power had gone with him to his grave. She was to be left hanging in the picture frame of wealth, a recognized reproduction.

There was nothing to do but endure the last drive of the day. She knew that when she returned to the apartment, the letter tray would be filled with formal condolences but the telephone would not be ringing. People could be expected to stop by and pay their last respects. But there would be no invitations coming in to small dinner parties in blue chip townhouses, or to join the trustees of the Metropolitan or some select cultural foundation. The servants would begin leaving, or stealing, the accountants would have to be watched. . . .

The chauffeur honked impatiently. She filled the back seat with stained white roses from the Chairman's grave. Her children were inserted beneath the lap robe. All the way back to Manhattan her silence was impenetrable.

"Buzz Mrs. Ryan," she said, as the Rolls emerged from Midtown Tunnel, "I'll need a wake-up call."

"A wake-up call?" The chauffeur took a startled look in the rear view mirror. "On the Monday morning after—"

"That's right." The widow was flipping through her date book, smiling, reckless with recuperation. "I must let the Board members know I'll be coming to their next meeting."

How simple . . . she would make it her business to have the president of the Resort Fund appointed quickly, and then she would give a testimonial dinner for the new Chairman . . . of course! it was simply a matter of looking at her new powers in another way. She would bring him out.

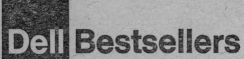

Dell Bestsellers